T0067324

REZ
Cheese

Elizabeth Wiley MA JD, POMO Elder

Order this book online at www.trafford.com
or email orders@trafford.com

Most Trafford titles are also available at major online book retailers.

© Copyright 2018 Elizabeth Wiley MA JD, POMO Elder.
All rights reserved. No part of this publication may be reproduced, stored in a
retrieval system, or transmitted, in any form or by any means, electronic, mechanical,
photocopying, recording, or otherwise, without the written prior permission of the author.

Print information available on the last page.

ISBN: 978-1-4907-8643-8 (sc)
ISBN: 978-1-4907-8645-2 (hc)
ISBN: 978-1-4907-8644-5 (e)

Library of Congress Control Number: 2017918885

Because of the dynamic nature of the Internet, any web addresses or links contained in
this book may have changed since publication and may no longer be valid. The views
expressed in this work are solely those of the author and do not necessarily reflect the
views of the publisher, and the publisher hereby disclaims any responsibility for them.

Any people depicted in stock imagery provided by Thinkstock are models,
and such images are being used for illustrative purposes only.
Certain stock imagery © Thinkstock.

Trafford rev. 02/07/2018

Trafford
PUBLISHING® www.trafford.com
North America & international
toll-free: 1 888 232 4444 (USA & Canada)
fax: 812 355 4082

REZ CHEESE written and illustrated by Elizabeth Wiley MA JD, POMO Elder

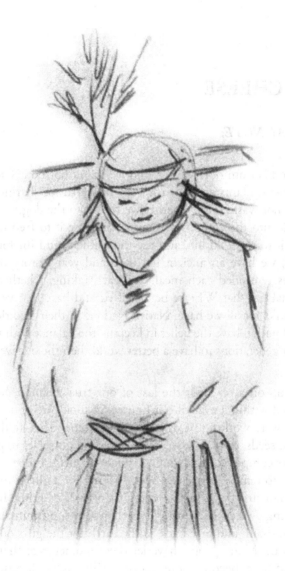

REZ CHEESE

SPECIAL NOTE:

ALL food is from our Creator, and we thank both our Creator and the animals, plants and our Mother the Earth for sharing with us. WE do not waste food, whether we feed it to the dog, or chickens, or put it into the compost container, and use it to feed the plants, or feed it to the wild life, and use the feathers, and fur for clothing and art, we have an ancient ten thousand year history of keeping ourselves reminded each meal, and each taking, whether of plant or animal life that WE are being gifted and have to give gratitude and thanks for all we have. Native Nations in their traditions, from EVERY nation have the belief in keeping the balance with nature for the next generations to have a better world than the one we enjoyed.

I grew up on a rez with the last of our true Shaman, he and his wife lived within a mile of our house and took care of us when our parents were working or otherwise not home. They told us when we plant seeds, or plants, we have to remind ourselves to give back. Whether compost or fish soup, or symbolic gifts of tobacco or sage, we need to remind ourselves we are asking for a gift of food in the future, not just thanking for the gifts of today, and be humble in our asking. When harvesting, whether plants, or animals, fish, or fowl, we thank and give back to the earth for the gifts our Creator gives to us. Many people have let these moments of thanksgiving and gratitude become rote actions, silly superstitions, or have forgotten them all together.

A thought I have had as an adult is that tobacco, and certain other leaves from plants sprinkled around where a new seed is planted is very likely to keep insects and birds from eating the new sprouts, because they have keen sense of smell, and will think it is left over oak and acorn compost, or tobacco. Whether ancient wisdom or not, it works in my garden. I often take the ashtray from my son's car or his smoking porch and pour boiling water over the butts, and make a strong tea, which I mix with dish soap, and spray on the plants to keep unwanted insects from eating them as they sprout and grow. The watering of the sprinklers, and a final wash in the sink remove all of the soap and tobacco residue safely. Usually the insects are starting to return by harvest time, showing the residue is gone even without the extra washing.

Whether a burger or some tenders, our children need to be reminded we do NOT waste the lives that were given, often in horrible conditions for our benefit. We do not have to go out eating twigs, and having lengthy ceremonies, but we do have to remind ourselves that our Creator is giving us sustenance, and show gratitude and honor those gifts by not wasting them. This does not mean clean your plate, it means at least put it in the compost bin at home or take it to the dog, and remind yourself to order less if you are constantly throwing food away. It also means do not take more than you can eat, or if you are not sure you like something, take one teaspoon to taste and find out, not a whole plateful. It means we ASK where our food is grown and under what conditions the animals live that end up on our plates and in the trash. If we refuse to buy products made with animal suffering and inhumane conditions, they will stop allowing it. Many markets and fast food chains now require that their food supplies are NOT factory farmed, and the animals are at least cage free, and not in slaughter yards prior to butchering.

The name of this book "Rez Cheeze" is in honor of the amazing food our relatives fed us out of whatever the BIA was handing out that time period. Whether you lived on the rez, or visited relatives or friends who had to survive with Treaty based Rez commodities, you have loved rez cheese dishes, especially rez cheese macaroni and cheese.

My Grandmother, and all of our Aunties had huge chunks (usually five pound blocks of cheap American cheese) of rez cheese in the refrigerator. Once in awhile there would be wheels of REAL cheese, those were saved for cooking with eggs, for sandwiches, quesadillas, and as an addition to the usual sauce made with the American cheese block for macaroni and cheese. Both kinds of cheese were used for yummy cheese sandwiches.

Many of our Aunties had sheep, goats and cows themselves and made their own cheeses as well. Most reserves did not have the opportunity for cows, but often had sheep and goats and made their own cheese. If you are fortunate to live near reservations that have huge reindeer, elk, moose, bison, or other mammal herds, you will have had the opportunity to eat the cheeses made from milk from those animals as well. The babies are NEVER taken from the mothers, just a little milk from each mother is taken for a few days, and heated and made into cheese and a very soft cheese that is almost likes sour cream or yogurt. These cheeses are in some areas left to smoke in the smoke house and kept over the year, cut up or grated into cheese dishes. As different cultures have married into the rez life, many of the cheese created is of an amazing variety.

In my research I found that most Native Nations around the world utilized the milk of the animals they used for travel and food. The Native Nations did NOT pen up animals, the animals roamed free, and what were called in a loose translation cowboys took care of them and conducted the ceremonies and slaughter in strict religious conditions so the animals did not suffer. Baby animals were left with their mothers, and SOME milk taken from each mother animal, which were given special treats of extra food for taking that milk. Some of this cheese and other milk products were traded with those who had other animals in their area. This subject is discussed at greater length in my book about Native Nations animal care. (The book and documentary video of "Horse Boy" about the last of the traditional Viking Mongol healers and equine therapists shows the lifestyle of the humans who live free with their animals, moving from seasonal range to keep the animals and humans fed and warm).

The next item was usually ten pounds of butter, in five-pound chunks. On the shelves were HUGE industrial size jars of jam, and cans of what said "PORK" or "BEEF" on them. Plain wrap existed on the rez long before grocery stores sold plain white cans and packages with the words written on them in plain block letters.

Huge bags of flour, sugar, rice, potatoes, onions were usually in the darkness of a cupboard since it takes a long time to use one hundred pounds of these products. LARD, another item that came either in five-pound chunks with greasy paper wrapped around, or in five gallon buckets. If it had been a good delivery on the monthly or bi monthly deliveries of treaty food, assured in exchange for not killing the squatters on the lands of the local natives, or in exchange for one rez taking on large numbers of refugees from reservations that had suddenly been discovered to have lush cattle grazing, or coal, oil or other minerals and the Natives got moved out by military troops, busses, trucks and bulldozers to make sure there was nothing to try and return to.............there would be giant size mayonnaise, and peanut butter. Once in awhile there would be spices, canned fruits and vegetables, often military surplus and also in HUGE containers.

The majority of the products were government surplus. As the United States had taken all of the land and water used for self sustaining Native Nations, the treaties ALL held clauses that said the government had to provide food for those on the reserves. Big farms and ranches got tax rebates as well as paid for supplying the products to the Treaty food systems and military food systems, Luckily for those large food suppliers, it also allowed them to keep their prime products on the market at higher prices by limiting the amount of those products for sale to the public.

If a rez was lucky enough to be near big dairy co-ops or vegetable, fruit, fish, or grain packaging plants, the products would be of better quality. Packagers like to keep their prices at least stable if not going up, and a surplus of product reduces the prices, so they would sell the surplus in large bags, boxes or cans with labels that said US Government Surplus on them. Hams, turkeys and after Easter lamb among other meats were often either smoked, or packaged in large cans, cooked in brine and labeled PORK, HAM, LAMB, or BEEF. On a lucky day, the cans might say SALMON, or TURKEY, or CHICKEN on the huge quart sized cans of meat or fish.

In some areas near newly developing frozen food plants, on reserves with refrigerators, huge white plastic bags marked in plain black letters "potato French fry cut" or Peas, or Mixed Vegetables. There were also plain white plastic bags of what looked like bent up opaque poker chips. If you put these into deep fat and fried them for a few seconds on each side, they would turn into yummy potato puffs that could be rolled in, what else??? Cheese and spices.

In the areas that did receive fresh produce, home canning was a big day on the days food was given out. Often the food would be one hundred pound bags of carrots, potatoes, onions, and sometimes crates of other fruits and vegetables. Family groups would get ready to can, and when the person picking up the produce came back, the girls and women, with the Elder women taking charge would clean and can everything and then split up the freshly canned jars at the end of the day depending on the size of the families and making sure disabled, or old people got enough to make it through until the next food delivery day.

On our rez, most of the people lived off the rez itself and many had small farms, or big garden plots. They would bring in crates of fresh produce to add to the canning day, everyone would bring their own jars. My Dad and some of the other young men with good off rez jobs would buy the wax, and/or new tops to make sure the canned items did not rot or go bad in the jars. Tomatoes during the summer and fall were in everyone's yards and farms and from diced, to whole stewed, to tomato sauces and hot chile salsas they were canned on Sundays after church at someone's home and passed around to the Elderly and disabled and those families with children who needed extra food. One of my favorites was tomatoes, onions, and mixed peppers, stewed for hours with whatever spices the Aunties had on hand. This sauce was then bottled, steamed and sealed. It was SO delicious with tortillas or oven baked bread, or even the cheap white bread in the BIA treaty food for the month.

Often the children and a few teens were gathered up with old paint cans washed out and supplied with a coat hanger handle if the can had no handle, and piled into the back of a pick up and went off to gather berries down by the river, creek or irrigation canals. Not all reserves had natural wild berry plants that grew in deep thickets for many miles. The children and teens would come back with more berries on their shirts and faces than in the filled cans, and someone would start cleaning the remaining berries for canning for pie filling and jams and jellies.

Often these big canning days were at someone's ranch after church or on Saturday while most of the men and boys were at work on their regular jobs, or doing extra time work at one of the local lumber mills.

The little old ladies would sit and pat our huge burrito sized tortillas and cook them on top of the wood stove they had at almost every ranch or farm just for the little old Aunties. The children would be helping, and hindering and the more jam they ate on hot buttered tortillas or fry bread the more noisier it became as the day went on.

After the canning, on the way home, each family would take canned items to the homes of elderly, and disabled, or families with many children to care for and drop the food off. We usually took a plate of the food from the pot luck served that day, and picked up the plate left the last time, for the next time. Our traditions were to make sure the young, old, disabled were cared for at all times. While dropping off food, a quick look around would tell those what needed to be done in case a roof needed repair, or painting or a ramp for the disabled needed work. The next Sunday that family would be on the list for the men and boys to go over and do the work while the women and girls were doing canning.

The traditions and manners related to this care for the elderly and disabled is well rooted in the humility of serving others. The tired children would be snoozing in the car while Mom chatted with the householder and Dad would walk around and see for himself what needed to be done. We would hear our Dad talking to his cousins and brothers telling them what needed to be done and where. It was NOT traditional to make those helped to feel shame or less for needing help. My Dad always made the people he helped feel as if THEY were doing him a favor to give him exercise and give my Mom a chance to talk to someone besides kids and him. My Dad, often on crutches, and casts from his many surgeries, and having to return soon, via two hour drive to the base for his treatment and his work for the motorpool while he was recovering, never made those people feel as if he was hurried to get home and get his own home and ranch together before he left to drive back to San Francisco, or to get to sleep for work the next day after he left the military and worked six days a week at a lumber mill to buy what he needed to support his family and build up his own ranch.

Most reserves, or farms and ranches off rez that I visited had home grown chicken, turkey, ducks, and some wild birds local to their area, but domesticated. Pigeons and doves were also in large supply as on a farm or ranch the birds would keep down the insects as well as provide eggs and meat. Many raised rabbits as they could be left out to run and forage for themselves during day time hours and would return at dusk to their little bunny barns and well fenced security for night time safety. My Dad would put out some grain for them to inspire their early and speedy return. Many reserves still had adequate herds of deer, antelope, elk, moose, and reindeer in the northern areas such as Alaska and Canada. I know today we were very fortunate.

Many reserves I visited during my childhood were surrounded by cattle ranches, the grazing had been fenced off, the Native herds of deer, antelope, wild goats, and domesticated goats and sheep were fenced out of both grazing and water. The rivers, creeks and lakes were fenced off for the cattle ranchers use, and fishing was no longer available to the Natives.

The most poverty stricken reservations were more reliant on government surplus monthly drop offs at the BIA area offices, or by their BIA Agent assigned to them. I will never forget them; they broke my heart even as a child who did not know even a small part of the reality of that poverty or the history behind it. Most of the women, as well as the men in our area had worked, or been in the military during World War II, and had saved and bought ranches and small farms, vineyards, and businesses. Sunday Church and traditional Pomo ceremonies and State or area wide medicine conferences and pow wows were places people also shared both fresh, smoked and canned foods or traded them.

On many reserves we visited over the decades the poverty was beyond heart breaking and beyond comprehension of a child. Without access to adequate water supplies farming was often not available. The water for drinking was either purchased by relatives who worked in towns and brought in by barrels in the back of pick up trucks, or in some reserves old horse and wagon teams. Most of the water for drinking was retrieved during rainy season and kept in old barrels scavenged at dumps, or purchased from wineries in vineyard areas. Otherwise the Elders, women and children took buckets and trekked to the nearest creek or river, hoping not go be spotted by the cattle wranglers who would beat, or shoot them for "stealing" water on their own Native lands, fenced off against treaties with the United States Government. When I was a child, it was a worse crime to poach deer or elk than to shoot Native women and children trying to get drinking water out of their ancestral creeks, rivers and ponds.

Bathing in the areas where water use was restricted was often a long walk, ride or drive for the whole family and done at the lake or river. Many homes had huge barrels of water saved from the rainy times, that was used in home made showers. Taking a bath each day was important. The water was then channeled into the vegetable gardens for double use. Often the children were washed with a wash cloth dipped into a hot bucket of water that had been heated on the back of the wood stove, from oldest to youngest, except babies who were washed with their Mother in clean water, everyone got washed, everyday, even in one small bucket of water. Each family had their own blend of local herbs and plants and used a variety of filtered lard from meat used by the family to create homemade soaps and shampoos. I loved those wonderful smelling soaps and shampoos.

It was interesting for me to find, when in law school, traveling to reservations around the country for research on Native legal systems to learn how many of the young men had been in the military and come home with the skills they learned of setting up field living quarters. It helped them set up showers, plumbing, and water systems on the reservations they were returning to. Many began to buy or build home generation systems for power as well.

Today most of us live in areas with water, sewers, electricity, heaters and air conditioners and a stove, no longer having to gather wood and use an old pot bellied stove for cooking and heating. But we need to remember there are STILL reserves where the people have to bring in water from long distances, and have no indoor plumbing. Many reserves that still DO use scavenged wood from the unwanted branches and twigs from clear cut forests that were taken by logging and never replanted for heating and cooking. The destruction of these forests ended the herds that had once been owned and managed by the Native Americans.

My parents met in the military, and lived in San Francisco until they were out of the service. My Mom was not a rez person. My Dad loved those big silver trailers, so he bought one and made sure we had water, and electricity and a sewer system, by installing the systems himself. There were wells that he dug out of the mountain on the rez to supply the water system. He got a job at the lumber mill to buy wood and the posts for electric and phone service at a discount, and to support the family until his ranch was making a profit. He constructed terraces and brought in soil for gardening as our Rez was mainly no a steep hill and very rugged and rocky.

His ancient Uncle, at that time about 103, helped him dig a well, and put in the pumps and piping necessary to have water for all needed for the trailer to be as nice as the house in San Francisco. He borrowed a tractor and bulldozer and put in a road where the car tracks had been so he could bring the trailer in, and went to work at the lumber mill buying the poles for electricity and installing them himself, then the electric company came and installed the wire he had to pay for. He dug and installed a sewage system which used rocks, and several grades of gravel and sand to clean the water before it got to the system used to water the plants in our garden. In the winter, when rain was often and heavy, he built the sewer system so it would leach and clean itself out each year.

Since both of our parents worked off the rez, we were raised by our cousins, and Aunties and Grandmother, as well as the ancient wife of my Dad's Great Uncle the Shamen, who spoke only the Pomo language. I would not realize for many years that most children did not grow up in two worlds. My Mother's family lived in Pasadena, California. Her Father was a retired Homicide Detective, her Mother a retired Dean of a Women's College, who had gone to both law and medical school, but her parents felt it was not lady like for her Rochester New York society heritage to work as either a doctor or lawyer. I have written a book "Selves" about the reality of growing up on a rez, and in a mansion in Pasadena after my parents divorce put the three of us into the back and forth marathon reality of children of divorce.

TABLE OF CONTENTS

RECIPES:

I have put both the old recipes, and newer, more health friendly recipes in this book: Research is now in progress finding that original foods are helping Native Americans to avoid or keep "the diabetes" under control. The research is also showing that the sugar, fat, and white flour the treaty foods left, and the current foods bought with food stamps or on reservation store shelves has created the diabetic crisis statistics for Native Americans.

Diabetes was called "the diabetes". It was a scary lurking reality when I was a child. When I was 18 I decided with one of my sisters that we did not want "the diabetes". Weight Watchers had just started a couple of years before, so we joined, hoping it would help us learn something that would keep "the diabetes" at bay.

Breakfast

Pancakes

My Grandmother, her sisters, and cousins, who we called "the Aunties" generally had, or at one time had had jobs in town, or in a far away cities, but they maintained their old ways of mixing up pancakes (as most of their recipes) using the "eye ball it" method of measuring, or amounts we children thought magic, the ability to pour something into their hand and know the right amount for amazingly good breakfast treats.

Depending on the reservation, and the poverty of the moment, pancakes could be as simple as flour, baking soda, and water, or complex, tasty treats with berries, fruits, and new cream piled high if the family had access to fresh whole milk. Sometimes the surplus box had some giant size pancake and biscuit mix and that was used to make the breakfast pancakes. If the family had their own chickens, geese and ducks, eggs were added to the mix.]

Once in awhile big packages which said EGGS on the white container sides came. I can still remember how nasty those dried eggs were, they were surplus from dried eggs sold to the military in most cases. These eggs were added to the pancakes rather than use real eggs. The taste did not make the pancakes taste bad.

Pancakes, depending on the delivery from the BIA, or on access and money to buy from town might be packaged pancake mix, or made from flour, sugar, butter delivered by the BIA agent. Either way was a great treat for those of kids visiting the Aunties that day. After foodstamps began to be used, most reserves handed out food stamps rather than government surplus commodities to the communities.

A general recipe:

Two one pint canning jars of flour (and sift it unless you wanted a little extra protein from bugs in those old days of BIA food disbursements).

One small fist full of sugar (you might want to sift that as well).

A big cooking spoonful of lard, or a slab of butter sliced with a hot knife off the five pound block.of butter, or melted out of a five gallon tub of lard by heating a metal cooking spoon and then scooping out lard from the bucket with the hot spoon. The lard or butter was then melted slightly by leaving it in a small pan or a clean can on the top of the wood stove a few minutes. When there was not enough butter, lard was used. When no lard, a slop of pork fat out of the used rinsed out food can that was kept on the back of the wood stove with left over bacon, or pork drippings. This can of drippings was also used for gravy which is discussed later with biscuits.

1/2 teaspoon of baking soda for each cup of flour The women and little old ladies simply poured the right amount in their hand and tossed it into the mix.

or 1 1/2 teaspoon of baking powder for each cup of flour (a canning jar of flour meant 2 to 4 teaspoons of baking powder, or a heaped teaspoon of baking soda.

a large pinch of salt two big eggs mixed with either a half cup of remixed powdered milk, canned milk, or a cup of real milk Stir together all the liquids After sifting the flour mix with the other dry ingredients (depending on the bugs, it was well worth sifting ALL the dry ingredients, including the dry milk)

Mix loosely together, do not over mix, lumps are OK!

Using an old tea cup drop by half cupfuls on the big greased up griddle, or huge wrought iron pan as big as the stove top, or often on the top of the wood stove itself.

When the bubbles start forming, add nuts, fruit cut into small chunks, berries, cheese cut into small bites, or grated, raisons, candies of many types were all celebrated by the children and the young at heart.

The more grease you add to the hot pan or grill surface, whether butter, vegetable oil, lard, or bacon/pork renderings from cooking pork, the crisper the pancakes will be on the sides.

When the bubbles are set, turn the pancakes over, and check until done, nice light brown, not burnt or raw.

Pile up on a hot pot or metal plate set on the back of the stove or in a warm oven, and finish cooking all the pancakes.

Serve with one of those industrial size jars of peanut butter, jam, or homemade jam and preserves, and either store bought or homemade syrup or honey, and of course MORE butter. Another great topping for these pancakes was a big bowl of cream taken off the top of fresh milk that had sat out from the last milking and scooped off the top of the bucket of milk, or out of the top of the cans waiting to be picked up by the dairy co op for processing and sale.

Depending on how many people were eating breakfast, and what they were doing, from shearing sheep, to branding cattle, to milking a dairy full of cows, or other farm work, or a barn raising, fixing either a house, barn, or putting in fences for an elderly or disabled person, or a family of relatives or just sitting around talking about the sermon you could put the whole jar of peanut butter, or gallon of jam on the table. The syrup often came in a quart sized white papered can that said in black letters "Syrup". This was often heated and poured into washed glass milk bottles, or heat proof one quart measuring cups and set on the table as well.

Another great topping for these pancakes was a big bowl of cream taken off the top of fresh milk that had sat out from the last milking and scooped off the top of the bucket of milk, or out of the top of the cans waiting to be picked up by the dairy co op for processing and sale.

For a healthier diet, buy a store bought mix that has all the ingredients contained and mixes with water. Follow the directions and look at the calorie count. Cook on a non stick pan, and serve with the fruit or berries only.

Some nuts and seeds are low calorie and can be added with the fruit sprinkled before flipping the half cooked pancakes. If you make your own jams and preserves (recipes later in this book) or use one teaspoon of store bought syrup, honey, or jam per pancake two to three pancakes is a good breakfast. Depending on the Auntie, and which ranch or farm was needing work done after church, piles and piles of pancakes would go down with a certain citrus drink that came in small packages and was always in huge jugs, made with as much sugar as bearable.

A childhood memory from every rez was the plastic drinking glasses bought at home sale shows, and yard sales, which NEVER gave up a slight taste of dish soap, but on hot, working days, made that drink taste all the more awesome and memorable.

Today and for most of the years of my children's childhood, I mixed this citrus drink with only 1/2 cup of sugar for each half gallon, and added both orange and lemon slices to the jar, no matter what the flavor on the packet. At my old age, I add lemon juice and NO sugar. I do not drink or use substitute sugar items. I have had this light summer drink for so many years now I do not notice the difference from those old sugared drinks of childhood. I also add a couple of green tea bags to the lemon and orange flavors to add flavor to the drink without adding calories. Lemon, orange, or other fruit slices also add taste and not many calories, if any.

For a healthier diet I also usually drink a glass of water before eating breakfast, and a glass of water with breakfast. No sugar.

Breakfast fry bread and eggs

When I was a child, everyone, even my white Grandparents who lived in a big city in Pasadena, a big city in Southern California had chickens, and raised their own eggs.

On every reservation I visited, as a child, and teen, and while doing research in law school, every household had chickens, turkeys, geese (often wild geese who had started out with rescued injured birds long years ago and grown into huge flocks of domesticated wild geese, often bred with farm geese of many breeds). On reserves without nearby water, the ducks, geese and kids would trek along on the morning and evening water walks. I was a city kid and it delighted me to watch the ducks and geese rush to the water, no matter how small the pond, or creek to splash and pick around with heads under water looking for good things to eat.

Many small bird flocks were also started with rescued injured birds and became large flocks of semi wild birds who roosted in fenced housing to protect them from the coyotes, wolves and wild dog packs among other predators, including the neighbors. The Natives had found that many small birds, such as small pheasants, game hens, pigeons, doves and quail if awakened in the night by a light, left on for half an hour would lay an extra egg. The eggs were often a variety of shades and colors, and sizes. A tiny hole in one end, a slightly larger hole in the other and the eggs would be blown out into a bowl and the shells used in art work. Broken and used shells were kept in the compost and/or crushed into the feeding areas for the birds to replace their calcium for egg laying. Feathers were used for art and pillows, quilts. Even the bones were often brined, then smoked and kept for winter when meat was scarce to cook as starters for stews and soups.

SO, eggs were a daily standard of at least one meal a day. Hard boiled eggs were generally in a bowl or basket in every household for the children to eat as snacks.

My Grandmother and Mother from Pasadena, and San Francisco learned how to make the bread, and then toast it on the open flame of a gas stove, or on a stick and held over an open fire, or just tossing it on top of the wood stove and letting it toast. In return they taught the others how to poach, and soft boil eggs to eat on toast. Before fried eggs, or scrambled eggs with everything in sight thrown in was the norm.

As farm children learn early, it is the duty of the children to gather the eggs early in the morning, the children who gather the eggs know which hens are getting to keep a group of eggs, and which are not. Eggs left here and there by the chickens are simply tucked in under a hen just beginning to sit on a cluster. Even a lost chick can be kept until night and tucked in under the wings of a sleeping hen and her brood, she will just accept it the next day since it has her scent and that of her chicks all over it.

The wild birds that live in fly away fenced areas, I used to wonder, did they come back and look at their nest and wonder where their egg had gone? Only some of the eggs would be removed, and my Dad used to whittle little eggs of all sizes to keep in the nests so the birds and chickens would not get discouraged at their eggs disappearing, if one was there, they would lay another and not get discouraged and fly away to build a nest in a tree. In spring and maybe a second time later in early summer the eggs would be left until the bird settled down and hatched them. We always liked finding bugs, and putting them in the feeders for the birds where we could watch them get them and fly to their nests in the nests they made inside the fenced area to feed their babies. If we found wild birds that had fallen from nests, we would just wait until night and tuck them under a sleeping Mother bird with her chicks if she had room. Those tireless birds would not seem to notice another gaping mouth the next day and raise them up as their own.

Fry bread and eggs was usually made from tortillas left from the day before at breakfast, the slightly hard tortillas would be rinsed quickly with a spray, or bowl of water, and then tossed into a frying pan, or deep wrought iron Dutch oven filled with hot lard to make breakfast fry bread.

Fry bread.

Across the Americas, Alaska and most of the American islands, fry bread, baked bread comes in many names, but it is the same (and yet different for every cook, and local culture) flour, salt, leavening, water mix cooked in hot oil, or a dry oven.

The two most commonly known are the lard, flour, baking soda, salt mix that is fried in fat, often called Bannock in the northern parts of the US and most of Canada and Alaska. The other is FRY BREAD, that commonly sold Pow Wow treat, flour, salt and soda fried in fat base for NDN tacos, and to put butter, jam and anything else you can think of on it if you do not have meat and salad for fry bread tacos. Both fry bread and bannock can be baked, or cooked like a pancake on a lightly oiled griddle or the top of a wood stove or the more easily recognized deep fat fried breads usually seen in pow wows and competitions.

Fry bread was of course, created from the surplus government food allotments designed to keep the bargains of the treaties so the Native Nations would not fight back and take their own lands back against the well, modernly armed armies and robber barons of the Americas, who had their own vigilante kill groups on "their" ranches regardless of the treaties and agreements of the United States Government to protect the Native Nations and their citizens.

The origins of the other tortilla like breads varied across the nation often made with wild rice, maize, of many colors, and even acorn mush, cooked in a variety of ways depending on the local use of acorn flour.

Again, using a favorite pot, old tea cup, or canning jar, the usual recipe is two measures of flour to one half measure of lard, a pinch of salt and a cupped hand amount (about 1/2 teaspoon baking soda, or 2 teaspoons of baking powder per measure of flour) of leavening and one measure of water, used sparingly to produce a lightly kneaded dough to create the bread.

Do not put all the water in at once, the humidity, the type of flour, and altitude make a difference in the dough. Add half the water, the colder the betters, and mix with a FORK until the it looks like cornmeal, then add water by spoonfuls until the dough comes together, and can be easily kneaded in the bowl. The old Aunties of my childhood could do all of this by experience and skill, not even using measures, just an old cup or clean can to dip flour out of the big bag. My Grandmother often used a mixture of flours, including her own self made acorn flour, or left over acorn mush added to the dough.

Those big flour bags, especially in the earliest of reservation days, were very important. ALL of the food came in either kegs, or cheap cotton material. The women took the empty bags, pulled out the seams, and washed the material and made clothing and pillows out of the cloth. The kegs were cleaned out and kept to bring meat, or more importantly to store rain water for use, since most of the reserves were no longer near to rivers with clean water supplies and irrigation and home use systems. Most of the reserves were not on lands with low water tables to be able to dig wells, so water saving was very important to a people who bathe every day.

To make breakfast, a fry bread is created, thick or thin as desired, and eggs are cooked and folded into the cooked fry breads if they are thin, or served on top of the fry breads if they are thick, ANOTHER great place to add cheese! Grated is best and it was often melted on the top of the wood stove in a can or small pan and poured over the eggs and bread if there was no oven available. In my Nation many of the families lived on farms off the reservation or in town and had electricity, gas, and appliances. Many others, even on the reservations (we have 22 recognized and over 50 total sub nations in our Pomo Nation) had electricity because once my Dad learned how to put in the poles, and rented the equipment to put in the poles and where to buy the poles and set them in, the people could have fundraisers, and buy wire and the electric company and phone company would string the wire, that meant washers, stoves and refrigerators.

EGGS FOR BREAKFAST

Many things can and were added to the eggs.

Potatoes, garlic, onions, mushrooms and other forest gathered fungi, fresh herbs, dried herbs, including self dried sea weeds and kelp from the old day recipes were often added to the egg mixtures. Many of the reserves we visited used a variety of roasted seeds from pine and other ever green trees local to their own rez. Whatever is left over from the meals of the day before. Clean out the fridge is a great egg dish made at Rez homes, with of course, Rez Cheeze on top.

In the ancient times, the days were filled with hard farm and herding work (there were NO wild animals in America, only managed herds, but that is another book) and making the homes and gathering materials for all aspects of life was hard work. In the dry seasons the women, children and Elders took leather bottles and clay pots out and brought water to the living compounds and to the plants, except in some of the winter long houses that had their own deep, cool trout ponds around them, with little bridges, gardens, and an array of water loving plants and herbs for winter use.

Prior to the lands being limited the long houses often had their own wells, and trout ponds or ponds with other fish, frogs, and crayfish to supplement food. Depending upon the area, many types of water thirsty plants grew along the edges of the ponds and were harvested as ready, or necessary. Water cress, and other water plants used as food staples surrounded the ponds, or were grown in old pots and later old broken kegs that BIA food was delivered in became pond containers to increase the plants growing in the ponds.

Before the settled cities were burned and the Native Nations had to live in mountains and on deserts to escape the capture and slavery or death of the Americans, most long houses and city homes had wells that ran into small ponds around the homes and cities to make sure there was always water for bathing, drinking, cooking and laundry. All of the water was then recycled for the gardens.

A heavy breakfast to keep up energy and a fry bread roll up or two to take along for a snack or lunch kept Native American people going even after the reservations came and took away their ability to self sustain on the land.

Meat and eggs

Meat and eggs is usually thought of as ham or sausage and eggs. In reservations the meat can be just about any kind of meat, including salmon that has been smoked and can be broken up into the eggs and onion, garlic or other vegetable and/or herb mixes.

As noted elsewhere in this book, I am not a confident wild food creator or finder, and admit freely that if I had to kill something to eat it, I would be a quick vegetarian. I am happy to clean it, smoke it, freeze it, but I can not kill something.

I therefore have in modern times been careful to either get my herbs, teas and spices from relatives who I KNOW know what they are eating and it has not killed them in many decades, or from stores that sell professionally raised produce or herbs, teas and spices. I also grow my own herbs and some plants in my garden, but admit readily that I would be very near death if forced to live off my own plant production or wild plant finding skills, I have none.

Mushrooms, and many types of bulb plants are readily available across the Americas and the islands, but I stick to those I buy in the supermarket. But they are great in eggs! Again, being fearful, I rarely buy any mushrooms or bulbs from anywhere but the super market, there are a number of Asian and other culture markets opening each year that sell different kinds of mushrooms and fungi. We ask shoppers what they think and how they prepare them. Another source of mushrooms without trusting myself (which I do not) out truffle hunting in the woods.

Left overs from the night before are a regular omelet fare and of course CHEESE in egg and meat mixtures for breakfast.

As a more healthy meal, two eggs, cooked in a non stick pan or with a spray of olive oil or butter in a wrought iron or omelet pan with low calorie vegetables, herbs and spices as desired with hot sauce and a sprinkle of grated cheese with ONE corn tortilla.

BREADS AND TORTILLAS

Whether dry cooked tortillas, or fried or baked breads there are many Native styled alternatives to toast. Today of course the three dozen commercially made tortillas available in one big bag are easy, but need to be watched for calories as there is NO work involved besides sliding your debit card to supply the family with excess calories.

in our Northern California areas, many of the people worked in San Francisco during and after the gold rush, passing as Mexicans, since Native Californians had a price on their head and were murdered and scalped for bounty paid by the governor of

California and bounty hunters sent out by the land grabbers who stole the state by murdering the Native Californians in their sleep.

Those who got to San Francisco often worked in the bakeries and learned to make the still famous sourdough breads and rolls. The sourdough bread and rolls became a favorite and were easily made after the BIA surplus food deliveries made flour, salt, and the ingredients to create sourdough starter plentiful. There are sourdough starters, both Native American and non Native that are passed from relative to relative and friend to friend, and back again that allegedly have lived for over a century. Native Californians who worked in San Francisco learned how to make sourdough, and also got their traditional black jeans, and black suit jackets by working in the factories that sprang up during the gold rush to supply the miners with clothes. The jackets were denim at that time, but over the years, black tee shirts, and black suit jackets became a part of traditional Native Californian daily apparel.

Most sourdough starters today start with 2 or 3 packages of commercial dry yeast, Dissolved in a cup of warm water, add 2 to 3 tablespoons of sugar and allow to froth up, about five minutes, then begin to "feed" your starter with a cup of milk that has been heated to boiling and allowed to sit until it is room temperature, a cup of sugar, and a teaspoon of salt for each 2 cup addition of flour. "feed" your sourdough each time you remove a cup of the starter mix by adding an addition 2 cups of flour, 1/2 cup sugar, 1/2 teaspoon salt and one cup of scalded and cooled milk. You can take out a cup of the mix and give it to someone else in a clean jar, or clean plastic bowl so they can start their own long living sourdough starter. If they keep it fed, it can last for years. Stir the starter thoroughly before taking it out of the original container. I have no idea of the health aspects of this practice, but many people swear their starters go back to the gold rush days. I personally put the starter in a new container (usually a big canning jar with top) from time to time and wash the old container thoroughly.

Since I was a child, either sourdough starter, or store bought yeast were the ways the rez flour /sugar got turned into sourdough and yummy sourdough breads were made.

In consideration of diet, and weight loss and diabetes control, plain dry cooked corn tortillas (I try to buy mine from either a reservation that raises the corn without GMO's or from Mexico where there are many varieties of corn, and no GMO's.) To also remember that two SMALL or regular sized corn and one flour tortilla are considered one bread serving, not those old stacks of both the size of the biggest pan available to cook them in!

In defense of the old days, when a person has to go out and plant the corn, and go get water in buckets to water the corn, and then has to harvest, dry and get the corn ready to make into tortillas, those old stacks of tortillas probably were not so fattening as they are today.

In the days of my childhood, venison, moose, elk or mutton, pork or beef left over from the night before were cut into squares and put into the eggs for the breakfast rolls eaten by everyone and taken for snacks later in the morning. Chicken, duck, goose, turkey and small game bird meat left over from dinner the evening before were also often added to the egg and potatoes of the morning meal. Whether corn, flour tortillas or half acorn flour breakfast fry bread, the CHEESE was usually present.

POTATOES

Many, many varieties of potatoes grew across the Americas and as they are easily replanted from the eyes they were a traded root stock and part of Native Nations diets, either grown or traded. Today there are a few groups attempting world wide to find and restore the choices of the most hardy of potatoes, but the five to ten main types of potato found in stores are the most readily available. Try other potatoes, in most Native languages simply called "root" with an identifying word to distinguish them from other root vegetables, or other potatoes. It is well worth the search of the internet to findgroups that are finding and restoring more varieties of potato world wide. They sell small packages of eye to sprout and grow.

One of the easiest ways to grow potatoes is to slit the sides of a bag of potting soil made for vegetables, shove in an eye and keep the soil moist, but not soggy until the sprouts come out, then keep them watered only as needed to keep the soil from drying out, the plants will begin to wilt to tell you if you have waited too long. The new potatoes in the bag may be harvested as noted on the planting material that comes with the eyes. I generally plant some of the new growth potatoes in the garden in spring and let them grow bigger potatoes for that and subsequent years. Many of these potatoes are so good they need nothing but a sprinkle of salt. The commercial market has to have crops that can ship without bruising and rotting, but it is well worth your while to grow less well used plants and share them as your crop grows.

A recent FNX documentary described the sad extinction of many varieties of potato, especially those multiple varieties from S. America after the europeans came to the continents. Often the potatoes were grown or would grow only in certain areas, and when the cattle were released, and the fields either plowed, or wild grasses brought to feed the cattle took over, the potatoes disappeared one variety at a time until only a few are readily grown enough for sale on the commercial local farmer markets.

Potatoes were roasted, and cut up and diced for morning omelets from those left over from dinner. Many other root vegetables were eaten and cared for by Native Nation farmers that are now extinct. We have found using different kinds of potatoes from markets fulfills our needs, but be wary of GMO crops.

During the Rez Cheese days potatoes were often diced and fried in lard or butter, with a hefty amount of cheese added at the end to melt on to the potatoes. Onions, garlic and other root vegetables could be added as well. Many spices were added to potatoes as the cooked. Depending on the Nation and who one's relatives were, and what Native Nations they were from this could be spicy peppers of many shades and heat, sea salt, regular salt from the BIA surplus box, cedar, nuts, and what are called loosely "shoots". These were tiny tips of many trees branches such as the many types of pine and cedar. However, as I will continue to note, I am not confident of my ability to identify these delicacies and there are some that have really bad effects on the stomach for some days, and some that if eaten in enough quantity, can actually dehydrate and cause the death of a small child or elderly person.

Besides the big burlap bags carrying hundred pounds of potatoes, sometimes in the rez boxes were often BIG white boxes labeled in simple black letters "Potatoes". These were instant mashed potatoes that became a staple of Rez cooking for many decades. Both kinds of potatoes could be added to stews, or mashed and made into creamy soups, including of course Rez Cheez Soup My Dad, and most of his Uncles and cousins grew, pickled and ate their own favorite hot peppers. These were either eaten along with breakfast foods, or snacks made from left overs from breakfast, or the hot peppers were cut up and scattered through the food as it was cooking.

ACORN, or other MUSH

My Grandmother and most of my Aunties made some kind of MUSH, usually acorn, or a mix of oatmeal, cream of wheat, and acorn mush they each prepared in their own way. Even in the same family, people had their own preference for preparing the acorn mush, and any other type of mush. The big pots of mush, sitting on the back of the stove were often the lunch and after school snacks for the children.

Cream of wheat was one mush that I remember as having been fried, when it was left over, and of course CHEEZ sprinkled over it. Sometimes it was fried on the same big grill as eggs, and each person would take a few pads of fried mush and some eggs, sprinkle some grated cheese on it, and eat it with tortillas or toast.

Our Rez was near many oak forests, and as children we went with our Grandmother and the Aunties, and all the children either too young for school, or out for the day, would help them gather acorns to fill the big baskets, or burlap bags each of them kept at home for the days they decided to prepare MUSH.

Oatmeal, cream of wheat, could be called mush, but everyone knew that MUSH meant acorn and the children knew which Aunties prepared theirs with more care, than others. If not properly prepared the oak tannins are not washed out of the acorn mush and can cause not just a horrible taste, I remember it as similar to when you have a handful of pennies, and forget to wash your hands, and get that awful old dirty penny taste,. Those tannins can also cause quite a stomachache as well.

MUSH could also be prepared with other items and cooked a different way and become part of lunch or dinner, or even a snack.

Most of the Aunties had their own blend of MUSH and herbs to help cure whatever ailed one. Like the jokes about "tussin.......... MUSH was not just a breakfast from time to time, it was for curing what ailed you. Some were so medicated they made the person well just thinking of having to eat any more of it. I am sure!!!

Some nations use the tannins from burning the left over husks of the acorns and filtering water through a fine mesh basket (or coffee filter today) to tan leather! Others used this as the base for many herbal soaps for bathing, laundry and cleaning the house or stable. Shampoos were also made with a little of this tannin water (which could also be created by burning bark and medium sized chunks of oak wood, putting the cold ash in a basket (or coffee filter) and washing it with water to be used for curing leather.

Tanning leather was closely related to both the burning of oak wood, and the tannin retrieved from removing it from the mush or from the husks of the acorns. The many many kinds of herbal plants and flowers that can be used to scent the soaps and shampoos are almost endless.

There is one type of chapperel, or what is commonly called sage brush, or sometimes tumbleweed, although these are NOT all the same plants, has the scent of a nice soap and cologne. In the times of Native Nations creating their own soaps and shampoos, this plant would add a wild sage/rosemary blend to the fragrance of the item. As the European cowboys began to spread across the lands, they could not always bathe will out running fence, or taking care of the cattle herds for the land barrons. When they went to a small town for church services, or out to a night out these cowboys would often substitute rubbing these plants over their body and clothes to disguise or hide the scent of not bathing and hard sweaty work with herds in hot sunlight. These plants often were named "cowboy colgne"......

Lunch

Fry Bread Tacos

Fry bread tacos differ from family to family

The traditional ones were not called fry bread tacos, they were often called fry bread tostadas, but today they have one thing in common, a piece of fry bread with meat, lettuce, tomato, maybe salsa, and cheese. The meat might be chicken, fish, turkey, goat, mutton, venison, bison, elk, moose or any other meat found locally, or in hunting season. Fish was also used, often smoked meat during the winter months when hunting and fishing were both hard due to the snow, or the animals being migrated away. The farm animals in winter are either bred, and getting ready to drop their young, or by February, if bred too early, already feeding and caring for their newborns. Except in the extreme case of starvation, the young were NOT slaughtered for food. People just got along on whatever was on the shelves from canning and from the BIA surplus food. Farm children know that if the livestock is killed for food, the next year will have even less food, so it is NOT used unless dire emergency is on the family and no one has relatives to borrow from. Except in the extreme case of starvation, the young were NOT slaughtered for food. People just got along on whatever was on the shelves from canning and from the BIA surplus food

Today fry bread tacos are often made with store bought tortillas, baked, not fried, or fried on a grill with a swift spray of no stick canned spray. This generally removes from one to three hundred calories per serving. The meat is often barbequed, or stewed, and low in fat, and the vegetables and salsa are all considered free fiber foods that use more calories to digest than in the item.

The cheese is usually grated, and only a small one ounce serving added. Cheese is a high fat food, so no more of the rez cheese days of putting a big slab on anything to increase the protein and food value of the meal.

his is important because fry bread was a large part of the problem for diabetic prone Native Americans. Often one piece of fry bread could have as many carbs as two slices of bread or a huge burrito sized tortilla does today Generally noted on the packaging as FOUR bread slices per tortilla, the fry bread having even more calories from the oil it was cooked in. The large serving of either lard, or pork, beef, or other animal fat, rendered and strained out from cooking meats, also added a large number of calories.

This is a great concern in the starting up of gall bladder problems which also appear to be a serious race and culture related problem for Native Americans.

Even the fry bread tacos sold at events are usually a lot more nutritionally prepared than those of the past rez cheese days when a SLAB of meat and another SLAB of cheese were the start of building the fry bread taco, and the salsa added as an afterthought.

Today a thin tortilla, baked or fried in no stick spray with 3 ounces of meat and one ounce of cheese, with more vegetables and salsa is a healthy lunch, but once in awhile, even if shared with someone to reduce the calories and fat intake, a real good old fashioned fried in lard fry bread taco with slathers of melted cheese is GREAT.

Acorn crepe roll ups

My Grandmother used to make what looked like crepes, she made them out of left over acorn mush, mixed with an egg, a cup or so of milk to get the consistency she wanted, and then smeared on a hot buttered griddle, or pan, or the griddle on the top of a wood burning stove. Sometimes she added flour as well to the mix. When browned on one side, she would put a line of meat mix, or maybe some fruit and jam mix, and roll them into crepes and brown on all sides of the roll. These were often served with grated cheese, salsa, or gravy. The fruit and jam crepes were often served with ice cold thick cream off the top of a bucket of milk that had been left overnight sitting in ice. No extra sugar, no beating, just the plain cold thick cream on the fruit and jam was delicious.

Goat, sheep or even dried milk, mixed with half the water and whipped with sugar make toppings for fruit crepes.

Dried Milk is another of the items that came in industrial size boxes, no markings on them, except USDA and the words DRY MILK, or MILK. One regular sized tea cup of the dry powder mixed with water in a one quart milk makes a quart of milk, usually used for cooking in reserves where cows, goats and sheep are herded and kept by almost every family. Dry Milk, 1 cup and one half cup of sugar with 1 1/2 cups of cold, cold water, or water mixed with ice cubes and whipped with a whisk or beater will turn into a whipped topping for fruit, pie, or crepes with fruit.

One quart bottle made the milk for most of those living on reserves with no grazing, or no water for cows. We used to buy milk at the store, or from a dairy and reuse the heavy glass brown or clear milk bottles, or give them to older or disabled relatives or single Moms with children when we mixed big batches of the USDA MILK at my Grandmothers, or one of the Aunties home on a Sunday after services.

I do have to admit it takes time to get used to the taste of any dried milk, they are much superior these days to those old Army surplus stock that were delivered to the reservations by the BIA in big white boxes marked simply MILK. There were also industrial sized cans of skim milk. It tasked as bad as it sounds. Once in awhile the BIA would have real condensed milk or sweetened condensed milk. The older children and teens would open the cans, put them on a burner, or the back of a wood stove and add sugar, and some spices, depending on the person making the treat. The result when cooked down was a kind of taffy candy the children loved.

MACARONI AND REZ CHEEZ

Good ole Rez cheese macaroni and cheese, like the Rez fry bread tacos was made with way too much fat, macaroni, and cheese for more than a small serving at a celebration or special meal today. In those days everyone had to work on the farms and ranches before and after school, and on weekends. Those who did not have a farm or ranch worked for someone else, or helped older or disabled relatives on their farms or ranches. EVERYONE played the radios in the livingroom, and the cars and trucks LOUD and danced while working, or not working. These huge meals with a lot of carbs were not so unhealthy as they are for people who are driven to school, or work, and spend the day with computers, phones and coming home to watch television or help the children do their homework on computers.

Most of the families had to go and get water either early before school or work, or after school or work and if there were older or disabled relatives living nearby, the children would be expected to drop by and get THEM water from the nearest pond or river before coming home to get water for their own family.

Rez macaroni and cheese started with a HUGE stew pot, or big metal milking bucket of salted water and a ten pound (or more, bag of rez macaroni. Usually in large 25 to 100 pound bags, simply marked US Govt. Macaroni. It was measured by quart canning jars, or a big washed out quart bucket that was used for the children to go look for berries. These were often old cans from vegetables, or fruit, with a heavy wire or rope attached for a handle. Two big containers into that huge boiling pot of water, often cooked on a cook stove, or the outdoor fire crane, or just sitting on two big rocks, or three bricks right on the hot coals.

In a big metal frying pan a one pound or so chunk of butter was melted, a cup of flour poured in and salt, and often onions that had been seared and pre cooked were added. Dry milk and water to make the whole sauce thick and yummy were added. Salt, pepper, and sometimes dried chili flakes made up the seasoning. THEN cheese of whatever kind there was that month was added. Most of the kids liked the cheap American cheese best, but often there were other kinds of cheese as well, just cut into chunks and stirred into the sauce until whoever was cooking decided it was the best.

The macaroni would be tested for tooth ready doneness and the water poured out. The sauce would be added and all would be stirred in and dumped into one or two big baking pans, covered with more chunks of cheese, or grated cheese, and crackers broken into crumbs, or corn flake cereal crumbled over the top. Baked until brown and bubbly and served with tortillas. Not exactly a perfectly healthy meal, but so yummy. Each Auntie or Grandmother had her own recipe, and most were not exactly the same due to the cheese available being different, but ALL a favorite of everyone. There was even a fake cheese dish if there was no cheese available. That had lard, bacon fat drippings left over in the can on the back of every stove, used with the butter and flour and spices to create the sauce. Then add the seared onions and macaroni, and put crackers or some kid of dried cereal (usually corn flakes, which also came in huge plain boxes marked only USDA Surplus CORNFLAKES.

No matter what pow wow, medicine conference, family holiday big farm workday or going to some Aunties home to repair something after church on Sunday. if no family member, the pastor would find a family in need, or to some disabled church member, old persons home, or single mother's home to repair something, the big community meals ALL had at least one or two big baking pans of Rez macaroni and cheese.

hen we were teenagers we were send on the Greyhound Bus to visit our Dad, or Grandmother at the rez. The big Greyhound station in Los Angeles was to me, scary early in the morning when our Mom put us on a bus destined for San Francisco, where we would be transferred from the express to a local and go on up to nearest town to the rez or whichever Aunt my Grandmother was living with at that time. She was old, and the diabetes was telling on her, so her daughters kept her at their homes to make sure she was cared for.

Those Greyhound stations had big cafeterias, or small cafés depending on the size of the town. San Francisco, and Los Angeles both had wonderful macaroni and cheese, somewhat like that from the rez cheez recipes. We would always get some while waiting for who ever was picking us up in Los Angeles, or while we waited for the local bus to load for us to get to our Grandmother.

My Grandmother loved those old wood stoves to cook on and heat the house with, so even in by then modern ranch homes belonging to her daughters, she put up a tent in the yard, with a wood stove and spent as much time cooking on it, and sitting by it as possible.

My Grandmother was one of the few who had managed to consistently escape the bounty hunters, on horseback, or in trucks with guns, who came to pick up the children and turn them over to the BIA schools. By the time my Dad came along in 1927 the practice had stopped, and most of our relatives said they were Mexican field workers and their children went to the regular schools or the schools set aside for the farm worker children. My Grandmother was functionally illiterate, but when she heard my Dad was coming home with an educated white woman, she got her daughters and grandchildren to teach her to read an write well enough that my Mother never knew she was illiterate. My Grandmother had wisdom and knew a lot about everything, she just could not read it, or write about it.

We of course, had a white Mom, and by the time we were of school age, had become back and forth marathon kids of divorce and went to school in my Mom's home town of Pasadena, California. My Mom had helped, and made sure most of my cousins were educated and had jobs so their children were either suffering the racism and other bias of the public schools, or went to private schools to get educated.

I knew, from visiting reserves and Native Nations across the Americas, including Canada, Alaska, and Mexico that many of the children were only educated as they could be by one room schools on the rez as the push to end the separate Native Nations was on, and many of the reserves and Nations were closed down and the people sent to slums to fend the best they could in a world they did not understand and did not want them. The minorities already shoved into the slum areas by racism and an unconstitutional self appointed elitist attitude in most cities, were NOT ready to let more poor people, who spoke other languages than any they knew take their tiny space.

My Mom wanted us to keep up with our own culture, so joined the SouthWest Museum and other programs such as the semi annual pow wow and dance groups all over Los Angeles County. She had some really good friends who were Chippewa from the Lake Superior area, relocated to Los Angeles by force, and we were mostly absorbed into the multiple cultures of the many Native Nations in Los Angeles. I do not remember many, if any, formal programs up north at, or by our rez. Many of my Uncles and cousins were born again Assembly of God ministers, and the majority of events were with the church. I do remember many :tent" revivals and ALL Of them had both fry bread and Rez cheez Mac and Cheez along with fish, abalone, sea weed, and a lot of fresh fruit and vegetables, venison and whatever meat, chicken, turkey, lamb that people brought to share.

MEAT

Meat, in the early fifties was actually pretty plentiful Young veterans were coming home and had money to buy little farms and ranches and had many types of meat growing on those farms. Chickens, ducks, rabbits were stock on all the farms. Turkeys on some of the bigger farms, as well as goats, sheep and even a cow or two. The big white 4H clubs sold off stock at the county fairs, and provided good breeding stock which the Native Californians had for the most part worked on the big ranches and raised for the whites, so knew how to feed, breed and care for. The Native American slaughter laws were somewhat I felt, knowing many Jewish people who kept Kosher, like Kosher laws, they required humane keeping of the animals, humane slaughter and health laws for salting, smoking and storing the meats and fish. Some of the older couples had the fish ponds around their homes that we were told by our Dad's Great Uncle had been part of each household in the times before contact. Trout and salmon grew in these ponds. Today most of the ponds still existing in my cousins homes are filled with expensive decorative koi, and not eaten!

There were places all around, as we went to visit cousins or friends, or accompanied ministers in the family to big camp meets on reserves all over the country where the dams and irrigation systems had cut off small lakes for many reasons, both salmon and trout would leave their eggs, and by late spring the lakes were land locked. The small fish were not subject to the predation and other risks that small fish in streams and creeks, or in the ocean if they reached it suffered. People who knew where these lakes were would take little tubs of chum from a bait shop or make their own from their own secret recipe, passed along by the elders of their family, and take nets and get pounds of the small landlocked fish. Boned and smoked they tasted like smoked salmon and were kept in smoke houses in baskets, or just in the kitchen in brown bags for snacking on.

The tiny salmon were often landlocked in their attempt to return to the sea after they were hatched, the Native people would gather them from those landlocked tiny ponds and put them into their own household ponds where they flourished on household leftovers and whatever grubs, bugs and other items the children found and threw into the ponds to feed them. The salmon and trout had the bad habit of learning to beg, and the more the family fed them, the more they became pets, and were not eaten. I remember one of my Mom's Uncles on his ranch, white man though he was, who fed his trout in the big ponds he had had made on his ranch. He used to laugh and say he had made them such pets that the STILL had to go to the store to buy salmon or out on a fishing boat to catch one because he did not have the heart to kill his friends for a meal.

Hunting was still a big part of Native American food resource near our rez, and there were quail, as well as many types of mountain, desert and sea birds that provided meals, As the fifties progressed, at least for our nation, most people had jobs and purchased meat from nearby farms, or relatives with farms, or the store in town.

Often the cousins, we still laugh since we ALL are cousins, and whenever any of us talk, we say my cousin......and everyone laughs..........but the cousins who were hunting age, or learning to hunt would often gather in a group and go off to somewhere that moose, elk, or other large prey animals were in season and get their tags, or not, and bring home a LOT of meat to be cleaned, packaged, and put in freezers. Those old freezers were not so great, and many people still had ice boxes and had to buy ice for them several times a week. Old traditional smoking and storage methods were still used. Today many of those who still hunt take the meat to professional butchers who have flash freezing capabilities and also professional sealing equipment. Even smoked meat is often taken to a professional butcher for sealing and storage preparation.

One of the fun memories of meat for my family was my Dad saying lets go to the beach, and off we went with paper sacks to bring newly gathered and dried seaweed home, and for my Aunties and Grandmother. He would stop at a market and get a great big steak, and would have the kids gather driftwood and start up a fire. We would all gather rocks, and he would let the rocks heat in the fire as it raged on the sand, as the coals became spread out and balanced, he would put a BIG rock in the middle and let it heat up. He would season the meat and then put it right on top of the big rock and let it cook, turning it once or twice with the big all purpose pocket knife he kept on him at all times.

My Mother never could believe that he could cook right on a rock in the middle of the fire and it came out clean, without ash, or sand on it. None of us have been able to acquire the great success my Dad had with this technique. Most of us, in our huge wrought iron pan, on top of the grate we bring to cook on, STILL get sand and grit in our beach day cook outs!

Fish were often speared on clean driftwood, or pieces of metal he brought for that purpose and set up at a slant over the edges of the fire to smoke and be readied for taking home and sharing with the Aunties and our Grandmother. I think his Grandmother was still alive at that time, and it was the duty of all the young persons to make sure these old ladies were kept in food of all kinds, and checked on to make sure they were being taken care of, or able to care for themselves, as they always said they were. There were few Elder men due to their having been lost in wars, or in land battles with those who swarmed into California for many types of gold rush.

My Dad, unless he had a cast on, used to dive for abalone, and other critters that were eaten, smoked or cooked on the hot rocks and beach fire. We loved the shells, and took them back to both of our Grandmothers. My one Grandmother kept them in her living room, just because they were beautiful, my Native American Grandmother had them hanging and in baskets with, or without plants growing in them.........she kept smaller, shells, rocks and all kinds of things children love to handle and see in those shells among her plants. Abalone, if larger would be pounded by one rock on another rock, then washed thoroughly in the ocean water, and either smoked for later use, or cooked on hot rocks or a big wrought iron frying pan. Abalone was also cut into small slivers and put into stews and soups which were boiled for hours because it could be VERY tough. I can remember, thinking it was like chewing on pieces of grated tennis shoe soles. I have never tasted or chewed a piece of tennis shoe sole, but for some reason that thought came to mind chewing those small pieces of tough abalone from a bowl of stew or soup.

Often the little old ladies and men came along on these beach trips, we just all bunched up tighter, the kids sat on laps, the tinier kids on those laps.They taught us how the old days were, and told us stories of their childhoods on these same beaches. There were tiny olive pit sized shells all along the beaches, the sea urchins and starfish poked holes in them and sucked the little snails out, these shells were so numerous they could be gathered by handfuls even when we were children and used for decorating clothing for events, and also for jewelry of many types, bracelets, necklaces for both men and women, and sewn onto headdresses, or strung on a piece of wire and used as rings.

The abalone shells were both whitish pink, pearl and one called red. Abalone can not be cut where the shell dust can get into your lungs or nose. The few who cut abalone would cut and shape it in ancient methods under water in a pool or large bucket. Today there are machines that can be operated electronically with the actual cutting edge under water, and all abalone carving artists use masks to keep the dust out of their lungs and nose. The large to small circles of abalone were used for necklaces and also as an exchange for items from persons who could not get to the coasts, could not dive for abalone, and/or were not able to cut and finish the abalone pieces. Tiny abalone shells washed up on the beaches, kindly already punched with a tiny whole by the starfish or urchins who had eaten the small residents before the shells caught in the tide and washed up on the beaches. Again, the children would gather these small shells and give them to the adults. They were taught how to create beautiful jewelry and hangings for dance wear.

Octopus and certain fish are often eaten raw, with rice, or acorn mush, or cooked tortillas of either flour, corn, or acorn. They were often eaten with hot peppers and tomato and seaweed salad. My Father did not eat onions, so no onions of any type in any of his dishes, but other relatives used either cooked or green onions, or other unknown bulbs, we saw our Aunties and Grandmother gather, but never knew what they were........they were usually called either "root" or "bulb". The reason my Dad did not like onions was that during the beginnings of World War One and then throughout the Depression, when the food suppliers to not just the American military, but the foreign troops were making a mint, food shortages hurt the Native American Treaty supplies, often there was not much in the deliveries to the Agent's office at the local BIA distribution center. My Dad's family had nothing much more than a couple of hundred pound bags of onions, they ate onion omelet, onion hash, onion soup, and even raw onions with what little they could find during those hard times. He simply never would eat onions again.

I do not remember ever eating squid, but they did catch them, and they too were eaten both raw, or cooked. I would guess my Dad did not like them. As a young boy, learning to dive for abalone, he had been grabbed by an octopus. One of his brothers or cousins realized he had been in the ocean for some time, and dove down and cut him out of the animal's legs. I think that is why he did not like to eat either squid or octopus, and why he always had a pocket knife, either in his pocket, or on a chain around his neck while in the ocean.

Sandwiches

The absolute favorite sandwich of my childhood memories was the cheap white bread sent with the government food programs and the cheese and BUTTER sandwiches cooked on hot wood stove tops. Of course many of my Aunties had gas, or electric stoves but my Grandmother loved her old wood cook stoves so most of the homes had them for her and her sisters to use when they came to visit. The big farms hosted most of the canning days, and the days of picking fruit and vegetables and shearing sheep. So, they had the best big woodstove cook days. My Grandmother and other Elder Aunties would make big tortillas, with cheese, or butter and big bottles of jam for the workers.

Even the small children had small buckets and were expected to go out and pick prunes, or fruit that had fallen on the ground and bring it back so the Elder Aunties could clean it up and wash it and make jam, preserves, jelly or juice with it. Nothing wasted. The skins, and other left overs were given to the chickens, ducks and pigs. The seeds were saved for a day when the teens would help plant them in buckets or fruit picking crates and compost mixed with soil to grow new trees for the ranches and farms.

Even fruit not grown at the place where it was being packed, the seeds were kept to grow new trees. Many times the teens and college age youth would all go together, early in the morning to big ranches that needed day pickers, and would pay cash each day. Besides pay which helped them buy nice cars, and pay for college, they also helped the family and saved towards their own ranch or home. They would bring home two or three big boxes or buckets of whatever they were picking. The over ripe fruit was often picked up off the ground and taken home to the canning Aunties as this fruit is much sweeter, and sun ripe to make especially nice preserves, jams, jelly and juices. As long as they did not take the prime fruit, the ranchers did not care, much of the nicest fruit falls off the trees, and is too ripe and/or too dirty to try to sell it commercially. The cost to wash and prepare it is too expensive to make it worth anything for a commercial grower.

Pear, peach and tart cherry pie fillings, and chutneys often really hot chutneys mixed with original blends of hot peppers were created at those canning events.

We might get a call, and go to someone's home when everyone was home from school or work, and everyone would help wash, clean and get that fruit ready to make juice, jam, jelly, or just add some to pies or fruit salad. We knew even then that we were much more fortunate than many others in America, let alone on other Rez, that did not have the farms and fruit and vegetable resources we had locally.

There were also mile after mile of a variety of grape vineyards in the Northern California area where while doing day work the teens and college age members of the family would bring back grapes for creating juices, jams and jellies. Some were dried on racks and made into raisins. Others were made into homemade wine. Today Dry Creek Rancheria has its own winery and sells a select limited amount of wine each year from the Reserve and at the casino events.

A little history of the sandwich itself is of course the story that the Earl of Sandwich would get so busy being busy at his work, or gambling, hunting, or fishing that he did not like to take time for meals, so would grab a big piece of bread, cut it in half and put a variety of whatever offerings were on the table between the slices, and invented the sandwich. Every culture has some kind of flat bread, tortilla, or sliced bread that has over the centuries built its own on the run meal in a piece of bread.

To make a rez cheese sandwich, a thick slice of cheese would be put between two pieces of bread, one outside slice buttered, and placed on the wood stove top, the top side then buttered, a pan lid was placed over three or four sandwiches at a time, and then they were flipped and recovered and let to finish toasting. Often mayonnaise was put on the inside of one of the slices of bread. As my Aunties and cousins began to grow cucumbers, more and more types of pickles began to be included in both the canning days, and the meals.

Of course two tortillas and a slab of cheese stuck on the top of the wood stove made delicious quesadillas available almost all the time at anyone's home. Most of the families who did not use rez BIA commodities would bring in cheese, flour and fruits and vegetables to add to the table when the whole family was on a work job after church. It now occurs to me that it is no wonder I LOVE Habitat for Humanity and Rebuilding Together projects which have a lot of people, and a lot of potluck and get things done for those who need it during great days of fun! That was my childhood.

Salads

Salads in our Pomo lands were great, from iceberg lettuce and tomatoes sold at the local market, to amazing creations of plants grown in the back yards, and gathered from the mountains and sea coast by my Aunties and Grandmother.

Italian oil and vinegar was the usual salad dressing I noticed as a child, with as many types of herbs in them as I had Aunties and Mom and Grandmother.......to create their own one of a kind dressing for the day. Today, with goat, sheep and cow cheese all of their salads now add in these often homemade nutritious bits.

Fruit was often added in to salads as well.

There were dark, tart cherries that used to be brought in from one of the farms and canned for jam, jelly and juice, small pieces of this cherry added to salad was a very good addition to the salad. Pine nuts, along with other nuts now purchased at the local trendy health food store are also part of salads on a regular basis. Seaweeds and kelps, gathered and dried during summer visits to the coast to fish and smoke fish and abalone for later in the year was also crumbled on salads.

SPAM was sometimes in big cans in the rez boxes, but generally the meat used for lunch was friend baloney, bought at a local supermarket, or friend meat from cans with white labels and plain black lettering, reading PORK, BEEF, CHICKEN or TUNA. In the earlier days of Treaty distribution foods big military surplus bologna and salami rolls, often five to ten pounds each, were part of the sandwich offerings for lunch.

A fried bologna sandwich was made by cutting a thick chunk of bologna off the roll, and fried in lard on a hot grill or top of the wood stove, after flipping a chunk of rez cheez was added and allowed to melt, then slung on to that cheap white bread, maybe with some mustard and enjoyed. Today a healthier all grain bread, thinner sliced bologna and cheese, pre –cut in store bought packages are often fried on a non stick pan and do remind me of that old child hood treat.

Anything left from the night before, or from breakfast rolled into a tortilla, or stuffed in between two pieces of bread is fair game for lunch.

As a child most of the men worked at the lumber mill, or driving trucks, or on the big farms and ranches around the area. The children and teens were dropped off at school when the men went to work, even if an hour or two before the busses came by the rural stops, or the school opened. They too had big rolls of leftovers, or two slices of bread with leftovers in them for lunch.

Today, with the concern for diabetic issues, most children and teens eat much healthier meals, whether sent in a lunch pail, or bag, or served at home on the days away from school. Whether carrots and celery sticks or more traditional foods, such as squash or pumpkin strips, jerky of a variety of home made types, smoked fish, or a sandwich of store bought lunch meat and cheese, thinly sliced, or leftover bison, elk, moose, goat, or sheep meat from the night before, there are many healthy choices for lunch bags.

Salads, soups, and fruit are often added as the bread, meat and high fat foods of the past are diminished.

For some years as food stamps came into use, stores made it a point to sell cheap, and fat / carbohydrate laden foods to the families. Today the trend is towards helping children to take responsibility for their own health and a growing understanding of the risk of diabetes in the Native American communities. Breakfast of chips and soda, or even sugar coated cereal soaked in soda are long gone, thanks to many Native American health workers bringing the responsibility of the diabetes home to the children, teens and parents.

Children no longer get up before dawn to help with milking cows, goats, or feeding the chickens, gathering the eggs, and other chores before showering and walking or running down the country rez roads a mile or two to the bus stop. They no longer come back from the long walk from the bus to more farm or ranch work, and housework before doing homework and helping prepare dinner.

They no longer either in the morning or after school, or both, have to take buckets down to the nearest river, creek or pond and get water for the day. They no longer have to daily gather wood for the constant supply of energy and heat for their home.

They no longer need those large amounts of calories and protein to keep from losing weight and keep their growing bodies healthy. Instead, obesity and the growing cases of type two diabetes have become critical, not just in Native Nations, but all over the globe. Now the trend is to utilize a return to pre-Treaty distribution foods, and pre food stamp store food. The nations are beginning to move towards a return to traditional fresh vegetable, fruit, berry, fish, meat and light breads, such as acorn or Native corn tortillas.

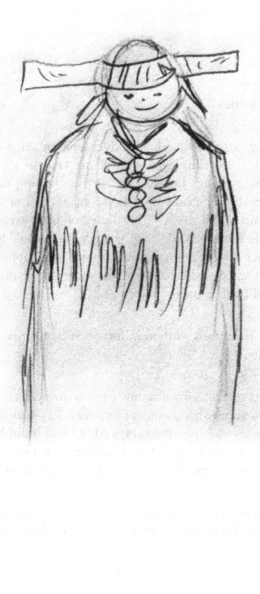

Dinner

Biscuit on a stick

Biscuit on a stick is something I discovered at some more rural reserves while traveling around with my Dad to visit relatives, or to go to what are loosely translated as healing or medicine conferences. Either made from home made mix of lard, flour, baking powder and salt OR big boxes of plain wrap biscuit / pancake mix from the USDA box enough water would be added to make a thick dough, and the dough spread, or wrapped in a ball, on a stick and cooked, over a fire like a hot dog or marshmallow turning until puffed up and brown.

These were then filled with meat, fish or chicken, or jam, jelly and lots of butter.

When I was sent to camp after my parents divorced and my Mom had to work and we had to go to camp for safety during her weeks with us for the summer, the camps ALSO had bread baked on a stick and made into meals. Many years later, when my sons were in Scouting, they too had bread on a stick and made them into meals.

Today the biscuits are often just canned biscuits baked in an oven, but it is a fun dinner meal reminding of the old days and traditions.

Barbequed meat

Today barbequed meats are mostly the same as those any other American barbeques on a hardware store barbeque, or old barrel smoker. In the days of my childhood, many of the Elders still cooked barbequed meat in the old ways, on open fires, with sticks stuck through the meat to hold it over the fire, or near the fire on one or two sides of the flames while cooking. Depending on what relatives were shearing sheep, or culling their goat herds, or needed barns, houses, fences repaired and produce picked and canned, the whole family headed over after church on Sunday to work and eat. If someone brought a few chickens, or ducks, or rabbits (my Dad raised all three and often brought enough for everyone) or goats, sheep or had deer eating the fruit off their trees, or a steer to slaughter, smoke and pack for the next few months, that meat would be cooked and eaten on huge tortillas my Grandmother and other Elder women made on the wood stove tops.

Native American children learn at an early age what woods are safe and which are not when gathering wood, the old folks were not confined by child abuse laws, and if someone brought poison oak twigs, or branches from trees that would make people sick if they were used for cooking or for the stakes to cook the meat.....a good old fashioned whacking would take place, and of course the cousins who had told that child to bring in the bad wood would snicker and laugh until THEY TOO got their share of the whacking, often with the offending branches.....which left one with poison oak as often as not, as well as a bruised, but smarter self.

Abalone (and other sea treats)

Abalone as mentioned earlier, used to be obtained in beach trips. Long ago a few days, or even weeks of summer vacation from the inland long houses gave children a huge playground and swimming in the ocean. The teens all dived for abalone, squid, octopus and other sea food to be eaten at the open fires pits, or smoked and prepared to take home for the winter food supplies.

By the fifties when I was a child, these beach trips were usually just day trips as many of the young people had returned from war with money to buy ranches and farms and vehicles to pick up the Elders and disabled or others without vehicles. The whole family would meet other families at the beach and spend at least a day, often a weekend camping, diving, fishing and eating, as well as drying seaweed and smoking fish and other sea food to take home.

Abalone is now fairly protected because of over fishing and pollution along the California coastal areas. Some of the Native Nations have permits and license to take a small number for food, but most abalone is purchased from seafood suppliers who rely on newly developing sea farming projects that do not harm the wild abalone and allow their numbers to increase as programs expand to clean the waters.

These new fish farming programs have also allowed artists a chance to purchase, or even just gather abalone shells that otherwise would be sent to the dump for traditional art and jewelry projects. For some years abalone shell, especially red abalone was endangered and not legal for use.

Today abalone is often cooked and eaten much as a steak. It is pounded between pieces of plastic wrap on a cutting board, with a commercial meat tenderizing tool. In the past the abalone was tenderized when removed from its shell, at the beach, with one rock, on another rock, then washed thoroughly in the ocean and smoked.

Abalone is also cut into strips and used in stew or soup. The traditions of every family are different in the preparation of these soups. Today pouring a can or two of commercially canned minestrone or vegetable soup into a pot, adding vegetables as desired, and shredded abalone and simmering for an hour or two makes a great, low calorie soup. Add leaks, potatoes, and/or yams or sweet potato or squash chunks and it is an old traditional stew.

Seafood stew can be created the same way, when the abalone is simmered until the shreds are tender, add shell fish, shrimp, fish of any type and some kelp, seaweed and vegetables for a hearty seafood stew which is amazing when served on a mixture of wild, brown and white rice to the taste of the chef. Some nations use pine sprouts, which are not pine sprouts, but instead are the new growth on pine twigs. I only use these if I really trust the person gathering the pine sprouts because some of the evergreens can make you very ill.

Pine and other seeds and nuts were usually dried and/or smoked, or roasted in a frying pan and stored for use in salads, soups and for mashing into meats for making jerky. If you do NOT know what you are doing, do not use them. Again, several of the evergreens can cause severe intestinal problems, harsh enough to put small children, or seniors and those with compromised immune systems into the hospital.

Steak sizzled on a rock

Meat or large filets of fish of any type can be cooked on a large flat rock. The fire is built up, whether wood, or commercial charcoals, and rocks are added while the fire is at its hottest point, as the flames begin to settle down, place a large, flat rock, that has been thoroughly washed on the other stones as flat as possible, when the coals have settled to an even cooking stage, place the meat or fish on the stone, and sizzle using a little bit of salty, and/or herbed water and oil, to baste as the meat is cooked for a few minutes on each side. The general rule is four minutes, flip over, baste, and cook another three minutes, flip and baste and leave for an additional two minutes. Then let sit on a plate, or hot pan for ten minutes to finish cooking inside. DO NOT USE this method with bear, pork or other meat that has to be cooked all the way through for health safety.

Steak sizzled on a plank

This method is similar to rock cooking, but uses a plank of wood. At the beach or river you might find a nice piece of driftwood that will work. I personally am not confident in my own ability not to choose a toxic wood, so either bring a relative who I trust their years of not poisoning themselves and the family, or a plank that are sold in some barbeque stores for the purpose of cooking meat. DO NOT USE treated wood from the lumber yard or you garage.

Like the stone, wash the plant, and let it soak in salted water, place on the stones when they are burned down to cooking heat, and allow the meat or fish to cook four to five minutes, flip, baste and cook another four to five minutes. The timing takes time, so in the beginning cut into the meat or fish to make sure it is done as you want before taking it off the fire. The plank makes an interesting serving and cutting platter, but be sure to put foil, or a piece of cardboard underneath to prevent burning the table.

The plant, if kept basted, and well enough soaked will not burn in those few minutes the meat or fish is cooking, but does smoke and add a wonderful smoky flavor to the meal.

Steamed and fresh vegetables

Vegetables were and are a large important part of healthy eating. Humans are not considered meat eaters, or vegetarian eaters, but as an original grazing animal, humans need vegetables and fruit for health. With the great amount of travel, inter-Nation events, and foreign fishermen and traders for thousands of years the kinds of fruits and vegetables in all areas varied, and grew in varieties. Some of the most ancient varieties are now being explored and attempts are being made to bring them back from near extinction. Such items as squash, potatoes, rices and fruits such as apples, pears and cactus fruits have traveled well, and been reestablished in other nations.

Baskets were used, often hung over a steaming pot of stew or soup, to steam vegetables. Vegetables were also simply eaten raw, or in salads as well.

Stew

Stew is a varied dish for every reservation, every cook and what is available. One of the most common stew is some form of meat cut in large pieces and browned, then cooked until soft with herbs, roots, and vegetables. Potatoes are generally added the last 45 minutes or until fork tender. Potatoes may be whole, or cut into large pieces, or diced depending on the cook. Roots consist of any local roots used by that Nation, or onions, shallots, garlic and parsnips, turnips or other root vegetables. Celery root, or fennel root are often used by modern cooks because they are available in the local supermarket. While not traditional, they do remind us that the traditional stews used what was local.

Soup

Depending on the time of the month, and the income level of the family, soup could be some wild gathered roots and vegetables with bones left over from meals, smoked and kept for the hard times. OR it could be big pieces of meat of any kind, or sea food, and vegetables, herbs and even beans and macaroni or other pasta served with fry bread or store bought bread.

Many of the Aunties, with large numbers of children had a left over "soup" that just simmered on the back of the stove, or on the wood stove, new left overs added whenever there were any, if the soup was getting too old, or tasted bad, it was poured, often into the holes dug for planting trees, or larger plants being put out after seeding in old fruit crates.

Sometimes the not so great soup would be poured to cool in buckets and given to the pigs, or chickens and other fowl or to the dogs.

Rice

Wild rice was a California Native American staple food, but after the Spanish and then the gold rush land grabs and destruction those wild rice, duck, goose laden marshes were gone, and the big bags of government rice became the staple rice of Native Californians. When the Chinese laborers came into the state to build the railway, they brought along their own rice and began to grow it around the state. The Japanese also came and brought new rice varieties over the decades. The Natives have had a nice choice of rice in place of the wild rice grown in the original marshlands of California.

Wild rice, as long as I have been around has been expensive and cherished, therefore mixed with another rice variety and used for stuffing meats, fowl and fish, or served with a variety of ancient traditional vegetables and roots, and those available in super markets of today. I like to buy prepared boxed wild rice mixes and use them instead of just one type of white or brown rice.

Beans

Again, depending on the time of year and the surplus of American farmers, huge bags of beans were delivered in the UDSA Surplus trucks. They might be pinto, white, lima, kidney or once in awhile even lentils of some kind or garbonzo beans. NOT a common use bean by Native Americans. Today garbonzo beans are a staple diabetic fighting protein in most Native American diets, and making their own herbs, garlic and cooked and smashed garbonzo bean dips for fry bread or chips, or vegetables is common on reserves that still receive some sort of government surplus food, rather than food stamps.

Like Humus, it is a high protein, low fat food that has taken on its own form with Native American herbs and spices from different areas of the Americas and the world being added.

Native Americans, similar to natives cooks from other lands, soak their beans and dried peas, or lentils at least over night. NOT as is commonly thought to make them softer and faster to cook, but to take the tannins and toxins out of the dried beans, or lentils and let the sprouting process begin. In research from weight control programs it has been shown that while DRIED beans, lentils and legumes are carbohydrate heavy, once sprouted, the proteins increased, the carbohydrate decreased in each serving. Many countries add lemon or other citrus juice to the cooked beans or legumes as well. Many spices, such as curry, turmeric, cumin as well as ginger, cloves, cinnamon are often added as new cultures have come to America and added their methods of cooking and serving legumes.

When I was growing up, the staple bean, often in 100 pound bags per family, was pinto beans. Of course the gassy problems associated with this bean created much laughter among the children and Elders, who seemed more afflicted than mid range age adults. The pre soaking appears to reduce the bloating associated with beans. Soak overnight or two days, to just as the bean begins to sprout stage helps, remember to rinse the beans and put in fresh water every five or six hours

Most families have their own methods of preparing the beans once they are cooked. Many mash them with bacon bits, sliced onion, garlic and some type of milk and cheese to create a smooth dip like substance that is eaten with tortillas friend and cut into chips. Often this type of dip like food was spiced up with HOT peppers, and several herbs and spices found locally to the person preparing the dish. This dip like food was fast moved from being eaten with hot just cooked tortillas and fry bread to commercially purchased chips of every type.

PUMPKINS and SQUASH

Across the Americas many varieties of pumpkin and squash are in the Auntie's or Grandmothers trilogy of seeds planted in the wandering and meandering gardens by the women and children. Today, due to the need to have pumpkins that will ship and not bruise, and not rot quickly very few varieties of pumpkin are still commercially available. It is well worth the time to go online and find newly cropping up "heritage" seed companies that have many types of many fruits and vegetables from the past, both those used by the Native Americans, and those brought in with the immigrants from around the world.

There are "wild" pumpkins that are so sweet that when cut and hung and smoked hold their sugar the entire year, and were used as candy across the Americas to trade and to please the children. Store pumpkins and squash in cool, not cold places, the cold of the refrigerator accelerates the change to sugar content in the fibers and defeats the purpose of healthy eating.

The cover photo is a zucchini lasagna:

Recipe: slice raw zucchini into slices lengthwise, it is up to the cook to decide how thick the slices are. Then blanche the strips in boiling water for four to five minutes. This depends on the type of zucchini, some soften fast, and need only four minutes, others need more.

Using olive oil on a paper towel make sure the bottom of a lasagna pan or other flat baking dish is covered with oil.

Put one layer of the blanched zucchini strips. Cover with diced tomatoes. You can cook onions in olive oil until clear, adding the tomatoes and any other sauce you prefer, some people use bottled or canned spaghetti sauce, others make their own sauce with a variety of peppers and onions Put 1/4 c. of grated cheese over the sauce and tomatoes, add another layer of zucchini strips.

Continue to layer, leaving the top layer with zucchini strips and sauce, spread another serving of grated cheese, any variety.

Bake at 400 degrees until the cheese is browned, then add a 1.2 cup of grated Mozzarella and Parmesan and/or Romano grated blend. Bake until browned. Cool for ten minutes and serve.

While not a traditional rez dish, it uses squash, and cheese and helps satisfy the hunger for pasta dishes without the unwanted carbohydrates and calories. Zucchini, onions, mushrooms (which can be added to the dish if desired) and tomatoes are ALL foods that take more energy to eat and digest than they contain. Some diet programs consider them FREE foods. The cheese is a milk, and a protein, and depending on the type of cheese may have to be considered a fat as well. READ the package.

You can use any type of summer squash, or mix them. IF you use winter squashes or pumpkin, use a mild tasting one, or mix, and one cup counts as a carbohydrate.

As a child every home garden, from my Grandmother in Pasadena, to my Grandmother on the Rez, and Aunties on their farms and ranches had a variety of squash and pumpkin growing. The pumpkins are NOT free foods, they are about 70 calories for each one cup serving, look them up in a diet food book before stuffing yourself with them. The yellow, small green, and little puffed types of squash are all FREE foods. Cauliflower is another vegetable that can be substituted for pasta in many dishes. Cooked to your preference, either raw, to overdone, cauliflower makes even pizza crust for a person needing to limit calories and carbohydrates.

Fruit and berry desserts

Fruits and berries are plentiful in the California orchard areas. These are great for desserts.

As a child in off months when fruit was not available, there were jars of fruit and berries canned over the harvesting periods.

Served with cheese and nice herbal teas they make great deserts.

Today the cheeses from the Northern California area are many and varied. Sheep, goat, and cow cheeses are created in small artisan home programs. In some counties they are not legal if sold, but the crafters will give the cheese away to those who come and learn how to make home cheese. A caution is that milk does have a VERY high rate of spoilage and listerosis, among other milk supported diseases related to it, so be very careful of where you buy artisan cheese.

In the market there are also a growing number of cheese varieties that can be used with fruit and berries for desserts.

Traditionally cakes, pies, cookies were made by each Auntie in her own style and always plentiful with huge chunks of butter, vats of lard, and those hundred pounds bags of flour and sugar available.

Most of the children had had their fill of berries while out picking them.

The adults enjoyed a bowl of fresh fruit after canning with berries added to the mix.

Cheese and cream

Traditionally cheese and cream for Northern California Native Nations were plentiful by the time the big herds were brought in. The Natives who pretended to be Mexican cowboys worked in the dairies and brought home milk, cream and cheese.

Many other reserves across America were not lucky enough to have had the invaders make the men and women into slaves to work their dairies, and could not pretend to be Mexicans, and were murdered for asking for a job on their own lands.

Native Americans were NOT allowed to work off the reserves, and often were shot or jailed for being seen in town. The women were often captured and put into sex trafficking today known as the saloons and red light houses. So they pretended to be Mexican workers from the missions or plantation ranches to get jobs and not get shot.

GRANDMOTHER AND AUNTIE GARDENS

Native Americans had what often were called Long Houses, these were where the women, children, and elders lived through the winter, and in parts of the year to plant for the coming year, as well as to store food for the winter. These Long Houses varied from city to city and were also changing as to the main source of employment and trade for various nations occurred. The plants that needed constant year round attendance were farmed near or around these long houses. As a child I visited reserves across the nation with my parents and saw many of the ancient and traditional gardens, wells were dug by the young men and boys when they were home, the women and girls kept up the water works, and irrigation for the fish and plants that were grown at the site.

A Nation that had huge herds of bison, elk, moose, reindeer, or antelope often had a community long house where the women and small children lived with the elders and disabled persons year round. The younger women and most of the men and boys went out with the herds to make sure they had great grazing and water to grow for the winter grazing areas which were not so lush. The animals needed to put on fat and muscle to make it through the winter. Many of these animals have 10 month gestation periods and would need healthy amounts of fat and muscle to not only survive, but to give healthy start to their unborn calves while wintering over. In nature, on a good migration schedule the men and others who took care of the herds took tents and passed by the long houses from time to time to make sure there was meat and fur, and milk for cheese. Many of the nations had for centuries been integrated with sailors who escaped foreign trading ships and settled with the Native Americans, they brought new ideas for cheese and butter production.

As the herds passed through the nations of other Native Americans they traded meat, furs and hides for whatever that nation was using as their main sources of livelihood.

The Native Americans did NOT remove the calves, instead they took a small amount of milk daily from the nursing mothers who were not undernourished while the herd was near the long houses, and made cheese and eventually butter which was stored for year round use and trading with other nations.

The Grandmothers and Aunties as the Elder women were often respectfully called, were in charge of the gardens. There are some huge, hundreds or thousands of acres of oak forests that originally were planted in patterns by whimsical women of the past. These women of the past left their mark, helping nature and the humans to come after them with their gardens.

By the time I came along the state was pretty much divided up into fenced off areas, and some wilderness parks. But our traditions were kept, even though the Grandmothers and Aunties instead of going to the beach or the valley to gather and preserve food for the winter on horseback, or walking, went in station wagons and trucks owned by their Grandsons and Nephews who when returning from war bought new trucks and small ranches and farms.

PLEASE, STOP DRINKING THE TOILET CLEANER

Excerpts from book and workbook for Native American treatment programs

I well know that it is NOT toilet bowl cleaner, but do not want to get sued by the manufacturer of the product that IS being used to get high, and do not want to help sad trend followers get in a mess by trying the real product that is being used to get high on reservations, and in poverty ridden areas. So in our programs, we call it toilet bowl cleaner and ask that our youth and teens stop drinking, snorting, or whatever they other antics they have derived to get high (and often brain damaged or DEAD) from these products.

The numbers of Native American youth and teens who abuse drugs and try to use household items because they think it makes them trendy is at a crisis level. Unfortunately the number of Native Americans who refuse to grow up or are so addicted they can not get free of the addictions they got as youths or teens is also increasing.

Sadly many of them are parents, and grandparents who teach their children and grandchildren at an early age to become addicted, and too often scarred for life, or dead. THIS is NOT our Native American way.

Often the teens and college students using these substances are thinking it makes them trendy. It often makes them dead, brain damaged, or in jail.

When I was a teen I remember a lot of drugs such as LSD coming into the trend category. One of them had a similar name to an oil additive for cars. It was often deadly for young people who thought the oil additive is what people were talking about as a "trendy" substance. It was NOT, they were too extremely different substances, the home made drug was not a lot safer, but a bit.

If you drink motor oil additives, you may have enough diarrhea to kill you. There was a kid in high school who DID drink a can of the oil additive, thinking he was the dude, he ended up the dud, being taken to the hospital oil spewing from both ends of his body and spending some time in intensive care. He survived, others did not.

I thank both of my parents for teaching us NOT to be trendy, and also for teaching us what reality is. My Mother ran the first drug clinic for youth in our local area of Los Angeles, and it only takes once to see a person on LSD laying on the floor, screaming and shouting that the walls are breathing, and going to eat them, to put taking trendy drugs right off your list of things to try.

BOTH of my parents wore nice clothing, of their own choice, not what the great "THEY" said you had to have each season, and both of them always drove nice cars, usually new ones. They chose their own hair styles, and took good physical care of their health and grooming. BUT they did not feel compelled to follow every trend and do what "they" did to be OK in their own lives.

One young man thought he was something that could fly, he jumped off the roof of his parents garage, another, rich white boy that he was, got into a fire fight with police and was shot off the roof of his parents home. Dead, whether from the drugs, or being shot, is still dead.

Today angst and trendy suicide thinking is also at crisis level. Parents NEED to talk to their children about these things, not just ignore them and pretend it will not happen to their children or teens.

In one lock down I worked with a SIX year old who had attempted suicide more than once. I asked him why, what could we as adults have done to make life seem so useless that he did not want it. He told me a few things, this was a rich, educated child. Someone had decided he had attention disorder deficit and put him on drugs, and he was smart enough to figure out that the great "they" had labeled him mentally ill. We brought him through this and he is now an adult, quite happy, who helps other high risk youth in his career.

I like to start with a sentence I had made up when I was a Sunday School Director long ago, I asked the children to make name tags, and then introduce themselves by saying I am WONDERFUL, because GOD created me, and I am the ONLY me that will ever be, and then tell us something unique and wonderful about them. Even the smallest five year olds could not say this simple sentence. It made me cry.

Being who I am, I just sat down on the floor in the midst of those children, and cried. I said that makes me TOO sad, what could all of us adults have done to the wonderful gift GOD gave us, to make you feel you are NOT OK. The kids loved it. I found out that most of those rich kids were also divorce survivors, most of them only came every other week because they traveled, often by air, to the other "reasonable" parent's home and attended another Sunday School that did not really want them. They felt that because most of the Sunday Schools, as their regular schools, wanted children to be there every week, and did not put them in plays, or choirs because they generally would NOT be there for practices and for performances. These children rarely belonged to Scouting or other programs because they needed ONE parent to take them as a priority and be there with them. We invented Lunchtime Scouting at the schools where each child had to BRING one adult, ONCE lunch time a year to talk about their life. From Fire Chief to on parole parents, the kids learned from each of those parents. Most of the teachers, aides and principals learned from those one half hour a year Scouting parents as well. Some children being raised by Grandparents who were just plain too tired to raise another set of children loved it that we helped their Grandchildren.....many of those Grandparents had great ideas and came and assisted in the children making their own costumes and often brought in great boxes of left over craft materials to help the process. These programs take only 1/2 hour every other week during school hours.

ALL the youth and teens participate at the same and equal level of their grade.

I immediately turned our Sunday School into an every Sunday for everyone program. Some of the non-divorced parents got angry, I had to have meetings and help them get the idea that if we are like Christ, the first thing he would have said is to "suffer the little Children".......and expect us to figure it out for the best of ALL the children. Even those who had it all perfect, the next week, they might have a traffic accident, or an illness, or divorce. Some of those parents were NOT happy that they could not have the seamstress make up a "perfect picture" costume for the holiday plays, and performances, but I thought those kid made costumes were the best ever. Having dress rehearsal one Sunday during service and the performance the next Sunday gave every child a chance to perform and be part of the program. Many of the parents began to become more involved and DID make costumes and sets WITH all the children, instead of competing at CHURCH to prove their family was superior in some financial way. When Mom and Grandma got to take a bow, and have their names in the program, drawn and printed up by big sisters and brothers and other family members.........for the beautiful and imaginative costumes and supplies for those costumes, for ALL the children, it surely was better than sitting out in that crowd thinking THEIR child was superior because of THEIR money, rather than being grateful to Creator for the amazing gift of that child to their family.

These issues are part of the complete book "Please Stop Drinking the Toilet Cleaner" and the KIDS ANONYMOUS and KID JR quasi youth self healing programs. The nicest parents who think they are completely reasonable are really surprised when they see how their children live life. It reminds me of a woman who wrote somewhere or other that she could hardly wait for her child to get old enough to go Christmas Shopping and was disappointed when the child was angry and upset. Then she bent down to hug that child and saw, exactly what that lovely experience was for the child.

A whole lot of shopping bags and fat thighs hitting them in the face and shoulders. That Mother saw herself, child's hand strangled in hers, after all, she was not a fool, she did not want to lose the child in the Mall. This woman realized that her old memories of a small town, and holiday shopping in small shops where everyone knew everyone, and the streets were NOT huge bustling uncaring thighs and behinds knocking her around that she had just inflicted on her child.

Parents who thought they were so reasonable with six months here, and six months there, or the back and forth marathon of children the world over, one weekend at one parent, the next at the other…no matter how that kept the child from building stable relationships at school, in the neighborhood, or even with other relatives.

The parents usually had NO TIME for their children, they often had to work, and go to school to support them and have a hope of getting a better job, and / or they had new dates or even new step parents, and step siblings the children had to deal with.

Many of these children felt NO ONE wanted them.

We worked with a group of teens, and invented a Twelve Step program, KIDS ANONYMOUS that simply said, I am a kid………we helped kids know that as a child, they had NO authority over their lives, and had to learn to survive if that was all they could do, their parents divorces and mental problems, and illness, or injuries, or prison, or death by accident or suicide.

It opened my eyes. These children had so much on their plate.

I had children in the Sunday School who were brought in by relatives who asked if they could stay a few extra hours because the family was trying to plan services for one or even both of the parents. I was often told these children were not behaving in school.

WE took time out and talked about the whole situation. The children were surprised to find other children also had parents die of illness or accident, and we learned that God is there for us. We read Psalm 27: 10 in which GOD promises that even if our father and mother forsakes us, GOD will never abandon us, and BE our forever good parent. Even parents loved that Psalm and what it meant to THEM.

Many years later, a young man about fourth grade asked me if it was OK to hate someone who had died. I said, well, I would guess so, if I had not hated my husband for his death, I could never have moved on and been able to remember all the good things about him and the good times we had and why I missed him so much. Children need more than being told to get out of the way the ADULTS have THINGS to do to "deal" with what is going on. AND the adults do not realize that while sitting down and really helping the child deal, they also begin to deal with whatever reality the family has to face, and live through without destroying their own lives. THIS is a very important part of veteran and active duty families. Sometimes the veteran or active duty family member has to go through treatment to be SAFE to be around the family. This is hard for everyone to understand and live with.

Native American children, raised in traditional ways do NOT have that attachment to ONE nuclear family. They grow up in the village it takes to raise a child. When I was at law school, I went out, in a four wheeler, and in my VW Bug to reservations where people still lived in areas where you drove as far as you could, then WALKED, and WALKED and WALKED to meet the Elders. I usually had teens and children to translate for me, as many of those Elders had managed to avoid the BIA bounty hunters and not gotten sent to the BIA schools, they spoke little if any English. These old folks, in their own languages told me how the old traditional ways and laws were, they told me how they adjusted as their lands were invaded and the genocide occurred on their nations. Often while translating the children were embarrassed, or shocked, the Elders had never told them what had been the real history of this country.

As many documentaries now show, especially from Canada, which has been more open and even apologetic about their abuse and genocide of the Native Nations over the centuries, the forced removal of children to schools where they were tortured for speaking their own languages, and often NEVER saw their own parents again. Treatment that destroyed those children was just a way of life to the government and non Native people. Many were even put up for adoption in the Nineteen twenties and thirties, the idea being that it would be better to assimilate them than to have to keep dealing with their traditional beliefs and culture, which were in direct opposition to the grab it all for just a few culture. Buffy Ste. Marie has some heart breaking material in her biographies and autobiographies of her experiences as a child adopted by a white family, who later became aware of the reality of the lives of the Native Nations people.

The psychological impact of these issues is only now being investigated in real research based studies. To many of us, it would seem a given, tear children away from their family, and culture, and torture them if they spoke their own language, or wanted to see their own parents and other relatives, and then send them off, expecting them to be grateful, as draftees to the worst military assignments, and to "jobs" that were in reality a form of slavery. I did research for a playwright from UCLA who was writing a screenplay about the Native experience at one of the most prestigious of those schools. It was horrifying to read what was thought of as GOOD for those children.

The discussion of these issues is necessary for Native American children and youth who are addicted and at risk of suicide. Besides the reality of drugs, the research appears to be showing that (White Bison Treatment Program among others) Native Americans need to find an identity and heal the horror when they find it.........added to the need for Native children and youth to realize that what they see on television, in movies, and even in video games is NOT how people really live, it is how movies make people to sell movies.

It is really time for YOUNG children to start to learn about drugs and how dangerous they are, and to learn that being "trendy" can be deadly.

There was a series of "Scared Straight" episodes that attempted to educate children, teens and college youth on these subjects. They were not supported enough to reach enough drug addicts and trend following pathetic cases to help enough teens and youth save their lives or stop themselves from getting caught up in a very difficult addiction cycle.

There are many other successful programs that have appeared and disappeared over the decades, it is time to realize that educating young people about trends and addictions at a very young age is serious and should be mandatory. NOT coloring books with little sayings, such as just say NO. It did not work.

The addiction treatment programs HAVE to be successful, utilize former addicts in helping others stop being addicts, not expensive programs with feely good group therapy that has been shown NOT to work in the long run.

Twelve Step programs worked because they were run by former addicts of many habitual behaviors that destroyed lives, and gave the honest and often confrontational help that addicts needed.

There are other programs that work in a similar way.

One HMO designed a program to help their patients quit smoking. It was based upon a self given survey that helped the addict figure out what parts of smoking that person was addicted to, or more than one.

One doctor had done a study on nicotine addiction, and wrote a concise report on the outcomes of that study, it showed that many people are plain and simply addicted to nicotine, given nicotine in gum, patches, or even in enemas, the smokers did not want to smoke.....but they did build an attachment to their new way of obtaining nicotine rush in their body.

Others, as found in the HMO studies, were addicted to the habit of using cigarettes for some reason.........instead of saying I need a break, and stepping out to calm down, which is NOT acceptable, they learned to go have a smoke, which was acceptable, and it built a habit pattern that whenever stressed, go smoke.

Native Americans tend to want to argue that tobacco is their culture and tradition. ONE pipe, passed among many, of organically grown tobacco for special events and ceremonies, is NOT the same as smoking chemically treated cigarettes that have been researched and shown to contain chemicals that make them MORE addictive than just plain tobacco.

A person might be tense, and like to take a break, but the HMO survey helped that person see that smoking was not the major addiction, the ease of saying "I am going for a smoke" was a lot less embarrassing than to admit the smoker was about to start screaming and run out of the class, meeting, or job site.

One psychiatrist did research on the "magic making" of all addictions. She attached the "magic making" to an immature wishful lifestyle that let a person run from tension of life, but did not resolve issues, therefore in the long run, the tensions built, so the person either got worse with one addiction, or added others.

This was often covered in her classes by helping the addicts begin to see how their behavior made no sense. Questions in their own surveys gave them the answers to start their own recovery. How many cigarettes (beers, sexual contacts, exercise classes, half gallons of ice cream, or pizzas, unneeded things purchased or gambling losses, hoarding of items or animals) does it take to pass a test, get someone to love you, get a job, get into a college of your choice, or change your health and appearance??? When a person begins to engage with their own flawed thinking patterns, they begin to not be addicted.

REAL addictions such as to prescription pain killers, diet pills, or street drugs such as heroin.

Every person needs to first of all admit that they are not in the habit of drinking bleach, or eating the cleanser that they clean the sink with. WHY? Because it is not good for their health, and they know better. Yet, they know that street drugs, and certain prescription drugs, especially if NOT prescribed for them, but purchased from someone else's prescription, are not good for their health, and they know better, but they use them anyway. WHY???

Each person has a different answer.

The groups that help each person admit that they have done this, and when and why they started help more than expensive replacement drugs to keep the addict from feeling the withdrawal symptoms of their previous addiction.

Some people are seriously mentally ill and need a good work up and prescription help to help them keep balanced in life. There are physical reasons for behavior, such as brain injury and chemical imbalance. There are mental and emotional reasons for behavior, generally having never found a way to function more successfully, or grown up thinking that commercials and music videos are real and how real people live.

Many people over the decades ruined their families by thinking that the "family" shows were how people really live. Especially for cultures that do NOT have the strange ideal of a man, woman and children who make it all alone in the world, to attempt to have that type of family by seeing television and movies, or reading magazine is NOT going to work.

Marriage is HARD, yet rewarding. Having children is even harder, yet rewarding. If YOUR family did NOT have that real prototype before them, they will not know how to do this hard, yet rewarding family work.

They need the help of serious professionals who want to help them HEAL, not just people who want to label them and give them MORE drugs.

Many people grew up with addicted parents, or care givers who TAUGHT them the only way to deal with life is with addictions of one kind or another. Groups and self help programs help these persons heal. They help each other heal because they grew up with the same issues that led THEM to addictions.

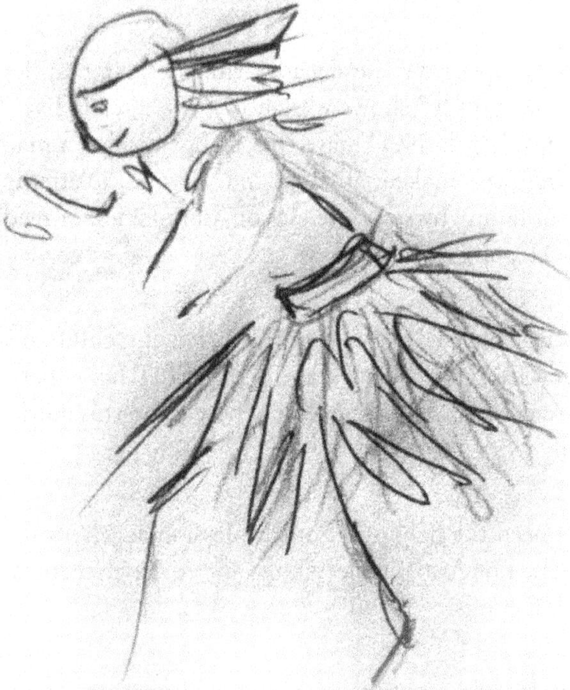

OGRES

Exerpts from Native Justice systems paper for law school class study on Native American traditional legal systems

Ogres was a very inaccurate translation of a word I learned for some of the juvenile programs of ancient and traditional days. Many of the nations had a similar way of dealing with children who were not behaving appropriately.

I found, over the decades that other Native Nations around the world had similar ways of dealing with their offensive children.

The Ogres could be an Elder, or an Auntie, or even a Dad, Uncle or Auntie. In many Native American Nations the family lived in groups in long houses, the children lived with a group of their Mother's family women and elders, and other Elders who were added if their own family had died off and they needed a family to live with. Especially after the invasions and genocide of America, children were often found wandering alone, or in small groups, these children were just included into the nearest long house. The men and boys who herded the animals for long periods of times often found both Native Nation children as well as orphaned white children who had through death or wandering off been separated from wagon trains, or pioneering groups. These children were also turned over to the nearest long house for raising.

The invaders wrote many a story of being stolen and kidnapped from families, but this was untrue, the children were NOT made into small size slaves as had happened to many immigrant children. The Mayflower, first voyage, listed bondage and indentured children that had been purchased, or brought along because the parents owed money to the family that brought them. These children WERE forced into slavery or indebted servitude, translated as harsh manual labor and abuse to make that a reality. It was NOT a habit of the Native Nations persons upon finding a lost child.

Each Ogre had their own amazing and frightening costume. I made it a hobby to invent little Ogre Dolls after I had gone to do research on reservations around America and saw some of the Ogres, either in pictures, sand drawings, or in pow wow events.

The parents of a misbehaving child would have Grandparents, and Uncles talk to the children, They would have other Elders talk to them, when all failed, one night, with a particularly wonderful smelling dinner being prepared a HUGE building shaking KNOCK KNOCK KNOCK would happen on the door posts of the long house, or single family home, or on the shield or name totem outside of a traveling tent if the child was out herding with a parent, or Grandparent.

When and adult answered the door, the Ogre would snort, and growl and sniff loudly and say it smelled a "bad child". The children all knew from stories that Ogres only liked to eat BAD children. The children who knew they had something to fear would hide. The Ogre would not listen to the parents telling tales of how all the children were GOOD children.

The adults would attempt to tempt the Ogre to sit down and eat the delicious meal now being set out. The Ogre would snort and growl and refuse, saying NO, I SMELL a BAD CHILD.

Of course the adults would convince the Ogre to take the best seat and eat the best food in the meal......the bad child, feeling very afraid that the Ogre would smell their badness

and eat them instead........kept hidden.

Soon the Ogre would stand up and rush around snorting and growling looking for that stinky bad child.......for dessert. The parents would drag the child out and say OH NO, this is a good child, the child would promise, admitting in the process what that child had been doing and asked to not do. Finally the Ogre would be tempted by a good basket of great leftovers and leave......... warning that if the smell did not stop, the Ogre would be back to eat that bad child.

The parents would comfort their child and talk about the warnings and disrespect of the family and Elders and how lucky that child was that the family stood up for the child so it was not eaten by the Ogre.

While today's psychologists might not think scaring a child was good for that child, in the context of the traditions and care of the parents and grandparents, the child usually did not have to have a second visit from the Ogre.......and as a younger child misbehaved could be counted on to relay their own experience with an Ogre coming because their stinky bad child smell had reached out into the world and brought the Ogre to eat THEM.

Depending on the Native Nation the Ogres had an unending variety of costumes and tricks to make them scarier. Big baskets of steaming smelly "something" that the parents were sure to let the child know was what was left of the last stinky bad child.........big hand carved evil faces with mouths that curved out and clanked open and shut, giant garish teeth glaring in the night were worked from within by strings by the Ogre. Tongues, often like reptile tongues were operated with strings from within and sniffed around the house to help nose out that stink of a bad child.

Many european nations have similar myths and called the beasts they threatened their children with Ogres, which is how that translation was put on the Native Nation Ogres, but the word, as so many Native Nation words are, was much more........it meant the terrifying eater of bad children......with a nose like the most capable dog, or snake that sniffs out its pray.

COWBOYS N NDNS

Exerpts from the book: NDN Rodeo: a look at NativeNaturalHorsemanship

Cowboys were invented actually in many native nations, and were NOT all male. Many a nation, especially after guns and huge conscripted armies were invented that committed genocide around the world, the Native Nations had to increase the jobs girls and women did. Many in fact became matriarchies because the men and boys would stay behind to let the women and older girls escape the deadly rapists and pillagers. They were either killed, or forced into labor to assist the army. BUT the origins of COW boys appears to be in Africa and India where before the empire builders arrived the young boys helped the men keep the herds safe, and learned the ceremonies, based on respect for nature of humane keeping of animals and humane and health safety slaughter of animals.

The Bible is filled with stories of shepherds, but there are also mentions of camel and other herders, and the "boys" who took care of those herds.

In some of the video material on World War II, Hitler's Nazi death march could be seen as they surged across their own continent. From old habits of genocidal armies of centuries, even millennia as shown in the Bible, the men and boys who were seen by the invaders as being worth some use to them, as laborers, or skilled workers, were taken by force and their families threatened if they did not go. In one video of the news coverage of a small town that was having a celebration, the people can be seen at a festival, little booths up, the church bells ringing, and then, said the ONE woman, severely burned and found by United States Occupation troops some days later they marched off and the remaining soldiers forced the women, children, elders and disabled into a church and burned it to the ground, the one woman had managed to go out a broken window and escape through the trees, the Nazi troops had marched in and after burning the people in the church, had crushed the entire town. The crushed town is shown in pictures and video taken just days after when the Occupied US and Allied Forces captured the area.

This was the attitude of those who came to the shores of America and all its continents. The cowboys we love in our television shows and movies were invented by Hollywood.

In a realtime history video replay of the first Mayflower created by a documentary company it could be seen that the history we have learned was also invented by some dramatic and self aggrandizing persons. In fact, BUSINESS persons, wanting to grab on to the lands and assets of the Native American Nations from the top of Alaska to the Southernmost tip of S. America and all the islands along the shores of two oceans paid for the Mayflower to sail. The Puritans DID want religious freedom, but they were inspired to sail by an offer of the BUSINESS persons who paid for the trip in exchange for contracts that the businessmen would own HALF of everything those travelers claimed, and built, and sold.

A very nice investment in SOMEONE ELSE's COUNTRY!

The emerging real history of the world is beginning to show a continuous history of greedy, uncivilized persons (which is what the Native Americans actually DID call those who arrived here, NOT great white anything as this book and many others now discuss) continually marching around the globe murdering the peaceful people and raping and pillaging to support their conscripted armies. It is called, among other things, the hierarchy of oppression......

The cowboys I learned while looking to study the history of Native American Rodeo and herding as well as animal care and its relationship to the ancient traditions of living not just in harmony with the earth and universe, were originally young boys, from Africa, India and other countries who took care of the COWS! Like sheep and goat herders, the cowboys were there to protect the free ranging herds of many people, and to protect their health not just for the current residents of that particular part of earth, but also for the next seven generations of both the humans, and animals.

LEGAL ETHICS: NOT JUST AN OXYMORON

Excerpts from Legal Ethics: Not Just an Oxymoron

Lawyers, at least when I went to law school, LOVED lawyer jokes. Just about anyone else gets upset, or at least feels disrespected by jokes about their job, gender, race, culture, nation, but lawyers and Judges I found LOVED jokes about lawyers. They would tell them at the start of classes in law school, they would tell them on the breaks, and the best ones, they would copy and hand out to the students.

It is NOT funny that Legal Ethics is considered at best an oxymoron, and at worst, a joke that is not a bit funny.

The law school I attended was a privilege. Lawyers and Judges as well as the few law school professors who were practicing lawyers or sitting Judges had proposed an experimental four year project and been approved by the State Bar to see if it might be best if only practicing lawyers in the field they were teaching, or Judges sitting in the field they were teaching should be the ONLY ones to train new lawyers, for law degrees, for the Bar Examinations, and for licensing.

One of the main issues was the hypothesis that lawyers trained only in school were not learning law, but instead how to play word games at the graduate levels. Lawyers have a whimsical Juris Doctorate, which although requires 16 papers, and 16 subjects to be mastered, is NOT considered a Doctoral Degree, nor a Masters Degree. A JD graduate, with a Masters in any subject is still whimsically considered equal to a Juris Doctor graduate. The word whimsical in this sense is carefully chosen. A student with a four year degree and a PhD degree has NOT mastered more subjects than any Juric Doctoral graduate. A Master's Degree is supposed to be teaching a student to research OTHER people's research and

APPLY it to research. To learn the rules of application of research by studying other person's research and seeing how it is assembled, and evaluated for ethics and professional research standards for the field being researched.

A PhD is supposed to be ORIGINAL research, either a follow up, upgraded application of the Master's Research, but with the student showing a firm grasp of the rules of PhD level original research, and applications of professional standards in the field, OR building new and higher standards for the field of research.

THIS IS NOT reflected in the refusal to address that a Juris Doctor is NOT considered a doctoral or masters level research student. Legal research, in the smallest case requires research and comparison of EXISTING research and proper quoting, application and footnoting or numbered APA standard biography for the paper. Lawyers have to learn to research existing material and utilize it in court and appellate work both ethically, and with a mindful attitude towards not using existing casework to bend the law in what would be considered a slippery slope in all other forms of research.

At the PhD level, most cases of precedence setting fact application or rule of law include at least an attempt to provide an ORIGINAL application of rule of law to the facts in the best interest of the client as well as justice and Constitutional rules and rights. The point here is that lawyers also have to learn the ethics and morals involved in utilizing facts, and existing case material with an eye to the big picture of the Constitution and the rights of ALL persons, not just to "win" a case for a client.

This book examines these areas of ethics and discusses morals in the practice of law.

The first DAY of law school, the Dean, who was a practicing Deputy Prosecutor in our County System, and the Professors who spoke spelled this out to us clearly. A lawyer is expected, and bound by ethics to protect the RIGHTS, not the wrongs of a client. Many\ lawyers want to argue that in fact they are bound to defend the wrongs or be in violation of their State Bar Code of Ethics.

In research for this book, I have written to every State Supreme Court and ASKED them for clarification on this issue, AND I have written to the Supreme Court of NOT just the United States, but other nations included in the United Nations for their opinions on this point of ethics law. The answers will be featured in the book.

There are certain aspects of law that come to mind each day as the news is reported. Tonight in our area it was reported that the drunk driver who killed a young Mother, and put her toddler into intensive care, no one sure if she will live, and left the rest of her family and children without a mother, wife, daughter, sister...... had been convicted of drunk driver and had his license suspended. While the State is charging him with a felony murder in the death of the young Mother, it is not going to help the family or children in any way.

Lawyers need to consider the effects of what they do. There are way too many lawyers advertising that they will make sure bad drivers who have gotten tickets will not even have to go to Court, let alone pay the fines, or do the jail time they deserve. Lawyers NEED to have a firm grip on where they move beyond defending the RIGHTS of their clients, and putting the rest of society at risk of possible death as in this case.

There is of course strong ethics and moral argument for the right of drivers not to be caught in quota scams, or profiling of certain drivers. In one area a group of middle aged women, all driving nice, new cars began to talk to each other, and notice how many of them had been stopped on a certain area of the freeway, and given tickets for NOT wearing their seat belts. In fact every one of them swore that they WERE wearing seatbelts, and had only unloosed the belt when they stopped for the officer and reached down to get their purse to provide their license and registration.

One of the women was related to a Highway Patrolman, who said, everyone knows women take off their seat belt when stopped, to reach down and get their purse before the officer gets to their window. He also said that if there was NO other reason to have stopped them it was unlikely the officer had seen if they were wearing a belt or not. His final comment was that they should get statements and take them to the area Commander. They discovered it was just a couple of officers that had stopped quite a large group of women. Each of the women had put up notices at work and asked neighbors if they knew anyone else stopped in this manner. It was proven that the officers were in fact just trying to pad their "convictions" because they knew that middle aged women in new expensive cars were very likely to have automatic seatbelts that would retract the moment they were released, and to have jobs which would make it more expensive to fight the ticket rather than just pay it at the DMV or Court or their own insurance company than to miss work.

There are arguments on both sides of the police/citizen issues.

However, lawyers need to not just be making a huge living off of bad drivers by putting them back on the road, or giving them the idea that what they did was NOT very serious.

Another area that really is bothersome is commercials for those who have been involved in big rig accidents to get big settlements in cases that often are caused by their party drivers who cause the accidents and then drive off, leaving the big rig and everyone hit by it injured and with huge property damage.

illustrations by Elizabeth Wiley

OTHER BOOKS BY AUTHOR

Reassessing and Restructuring Public Agencies: What to do to save our Country

Carousel Horse-a teaching inclusive book about equine therapy

Could This Be Magic- a VERY short book about the time I spent with VAN HALEN Dollars in the Streets-Lydia Caceres Edited by Author about first woman horse trainer at Belmont Park

Addicted to Dick –a healing book quasi Twelve Step for women with addiction to mean men

Books to be released:

Carousel Two: Equine therapy for veterans

Still Spinning: Equine therapy for women veterans

Legal Ethics: An Oxymoron???

Spirit Horse II: Equine therapy manuals and workbooks

Kids Anonymous and Kids Jr. quasi twelve step books for and by youth and teens

12 Steps Back from Betrayal from Brothers at Arms and 12 Steps Home two quasi twelve step books and work books created by author and veterans, and author's Father for Native American and other veterans

BIG LIZ: The Leader of the Gang Racial Tension and Gang Abatement work by author